A LEADERSHIP EXPERIENCE

Patty Hendrickson™

INSPIRING LEADERS

ISBN-13: 978-1-7353446-0-7

This guide is available at special discounts when purchased in bulk for premiums, fundraising or educational use. Special editions or excerpts can also be created to specifications of themes and organizational jargon. For details contact Patty@PattyHendrickson.com.

Patty Hendrickson
President & Certified Speaking Professional
Hendrickson Leadership Group, Inc.
La Crosse, WI 54601
Patty@PattyHendrickson.com

Patty Hendrickson™

INSPIRING LEADERS

**Patty Hendrickson
Hendrickson Leadership Group, Inc.
La Crosse, WI 54601
Patty@PattyHendrickson.com**

Dear Leader,

Welcome to **A Leadership Experience!**

This collection of inspirational messages and leadership tools is designed just for you. Whether you're a new member starting your personal leadership experience, a seasoned officer, or an eager student of leadership, this is a resource for you.

To get the most out of this tool, spend some peaceful time browsing these pages. The more familiar you become with this resource, the more helpful you will find it. Feel free to make it your own. Write or make notes throughout the guide. Mark the places where you found something that you want to use as a resource. If you find some other wonderful inspirational items, keep them in the back of the guide. However you choose to use this tool, make it your own.

As Fred Rogers or "Mr. Rogers" said, **"As human beings, our job in life is to help people realize how rare and valuable each one of us really is, that each of us has something that no one else has, or ever will have, something inside that is unique to all time. It's our job to encourage each other to discover that uniqueness and to provide ways of developing its expression."**

Have faith in the special qualities you have to make a difference in the world. Enjoy your leadership experience!

Enthusiastically,

Patty Hendrickson

About
Patty Hendrickson

Patty Hendrickson, MBA, CSP is President of Hendrickson Leadership Group and she is forever a student of leadership development.

She is a booked and busy speaker who delivers high-energy and highly interactive keynotes and leadership training sessions on a variety of topics such as engagement, team building, positivity and motivation.

Patty is a product of Career and Technical Student Organizations (CTSOs) serving as a local, state and national president. She continues to teach, train, and inspire thousands of state and national CTSO leadership teams to leave a legacy.

As a past collegiate sorority leader and student government officer, she continues to deliver highly engaging programs on campuses throughout America helping leaders fulfill a bigger purpose to enrich the lives of their members. Patty also serves as a Chapter Advisor for an Alpha Phi Chapter which continues to maintain a full roster of active members and a committed Advisory Board.

As an award-winning organizational leader, she understands the magic of engagement. The legacy of each team member needs to be honored and celebrated. The culture we build is an intentional result of bringing the gifts and talents of everyone together in a big, bold mosaic.

Patty's lively delivery style with purposeful engagement (and usually NO PowerPoint) is a welcomed breath of fresh air for both corporate and association audiences.

When she isn't working, Patty enjoys exploring the beauty of her community in the bluffs of Wisconsin with her husband and two children. As an avid sports enthusiast - particularly a football and collegiate basketball fan, you'll also find her wearing a team jersey on every game day.

Visit www.pattyhendrickson.com for more information on programs and services offered by Patty Hendrickson.

Table of Contents

SELF-LEADERSHIP

Patty Hendrickson™

INSPIRING LEADERS

The Leadership Starter Kit

Yes! Elections are very exciting! Whether you were selected or elected, you have a term of office to give your best. Your organization probably has an itemized list of duties and responsibilities. These are the things your organization says you need to achieve. But there is another special list. It's the Leadership Starter Kit.

The Leadership Starter Kit lists six items you need to know and use every day. These are six practices that will help you and your team stand out.

- Keep Learning
- Engage Members
- Be Interested, Not Interesting
- Practice a Host Attitude
- Be YOUR best, not THE best
- Replace Yourself

Keep Learning

As an elected officer, you've probably served in other elected roles. And you're probably looked upon as an initiator because you often make things happen. And people appreciate that you have your "act together." You aren't often showing up bragging about your mistakes or failures. As a member of a team it is important to keep trying new things in new ways. Some times that means making mistakes. Your team needs to make it your ordinary practice to talk about both your successes and setbacks.

> "The greatest mistake you can make in life is to be continually fearing you will make one."
> – Elbert Hubbard

If you've been trying to tackle a project and found some ways that didn't work, we should show up and share that with the rest of our team. And of course, share the way that you successfully completed projects. Learning and growing with all it's joy and frustration is something that shows your willingness to try new things.

Engage Members

You are the ambassador and the chief cheerleader for all members. The number one job of all officers is to recruit and retain your membership. That means finding ways for our members to fall in love with the organization all over again. Highlighting and celebrating wonderful moments of our members on social media platforms. Publicly announcing members and chapter successes at meetings and conferences. Any way we can spotlight member success shows we value and admire what they are doing for the organization.

20 Feet Apart. At live events it's very important for the officer team to be "member" focused and not "team" focused. Far too often an officer team comes together after not seeing one another for a long time and everyone is so excited to see each other. The team huddles up and shares their most recent news. That's fine. But the moment the first member shows up, the officer team should disperse or scatter. When any members show up you should be no less than 20 feet apart. You can socialize with your team later. At an event – it's all about engaging the members.

The Connection Formula. At any live event the officer team needs to connect with as many members as possible. You want everyone to feel that they were personally welcomed to the event. And there is a formula to make this happen. (Number of Attendees) divided by (Number of Officers). If the Fall Leadership Conference will have 1500 attendees and there are 10 officers, that means every officer needs to smile at, shake hands with, or welcome 150 members. This is a critical step to build the excitement and engagement at the conference.

This is also why officers need to show up as ready as possible. Officers shouldn't be worried about logistics. They should be there to be the most gracious hosts possible for the members. If every attendee is greeted in some way, the energy at the event will definitely be higher and people will feel that they have connected with others.

10/5 Rule. Many large organizations with impeccable customer service have implemented the 10/5 Rule because it works. Every time a person is within 10 feet of you, you should smile, look them in the eye, or nod at them. You are acknowledging that you see them. Every time a person is within 5 feet of you, you should connect with them with a handshake or a "hello." The 10/5 Rule creates an environment where people feel welcomed.

Be Interested, Not Interesting

You show up to engage with members and learn about them. You might do a lot for the organization, but you want to let the members shine. If you're worried about being interested, your focus is on yourself. Others can tell when you are somewhat self-absorbed. The best way to show you are interested is by asking questions. Asking "what" and "how" questions that require more than a one-word answer is a terrific way to start conversations about others. If you're someone who is a bit more reserved, don't be stressed about striking up conversations. Show up with a list of three or four questions you can ask others. This is a terrific way to get the attention off of you and onto others. Open the conversation and let them start talking about their own experiences.

Practice a Host Attitude

So often when officers come together to re-group they huddle up in a circle and start sharing their latest adventures with one another. They are extremely focused on each other and not very inclusive. Officers in particular need to set the tone as a welcoming force for everyone. Avoid creating a tight circle that looks like a bagel. Instead, we need to leave a safe place for others to land and feel included. "Don't be a bagel, be a croissant." Instead of the closed bagel, open up the circle like a croissant. You'll be a much more welcoming place for members to join in your conversation.

Be Your Best, Not The Best

"Comparison is the thief of joy" is a beautiful quote by President Teddy Roosevelt. We often compare ourselves to others and sometimes feel inadequate or less than. Every person is born with a unique basket of gifts. These are skills and attributes you bring to the world. Every person needs to use their talents and gifts to the best of their ability. Hiding or ignoring some of your gifts cheats the world out of your wonderful. Encourage members of your team to share the things that make them feel empowered and strong. When everyone brings their best, the team is functioning at a very high level.

Replace Yourself

At the start of your term it seems you will have a l-o-n-g time to serve, but it goes by very quickly. One of your major responsibilities is to replace yourself. This is called succession planning. You want the organization to grow. You need to find and encourage other strong and willing members to run for office. Find at least two individuals to run for state or national office.

When you show up at events in your official uniform people are very impressed by being with a state or national officer. Consider every time you are with some outstanding members you have the ability to encourage them. Yes! You do have the ability to encourage them. It's as if you have a little magical dust and every time you share praise about a member or say encouraging thoughts about them you are sprinkling that magical dust upon them. Imagine how wonderful you would make a stellar local member feel if you simply said something like, "Wow, you do great work! You should consider running for office." Now that's planting seeds for people to think about the possibilities.

Build Your Presentation

Congratulations! You were asked to present. How exciting!

It's an honor to be asked to present. Immediately your mind starts to wander generating ideas. Your energy level is high. Here is a non-traditional smart process to build a strong presentation.

Steps to Build a Presentation

Questions and More Questions
Topic
Objectives
Close
Opening
Body
Personal Polish
Natural Delivery
Documentation
Monumental Miscellaneous

Questions and More Questions

Ask yourself some important questions.

Why have I been asked to speak?

You may be the only officer at the event. Or the meeting planner may want to showcase your talents in front of other members. Ask the planner why they want you to speak. Meeting the needs of the planner is a great place to start.

Who will be in the audience?

The information you share with educators will be different than what you share with students. The information you share with enthusiastic and experienced chapter officers will be different than what you share with just members.

What do I have to offer the audience?

This is the most important question. The audience must believe you are qualified to share the topic. An audience wouldn't believe you're qualified to share the topic "Today's Corporate World." But you are very credible sharing "Officer Responsibilities – The Real Story." You must have experience or knowledge of your topic. Credibility is essential for you to share a strong message.

Remember that credibility equals believability.

Discovering your credibility is important and relatively easy. Create your "Credibility Source List." This is simply a list of everything you do and know. It's your knowledge and experience. Your list might include: elected officer, social media chair, singer, skateboarder, accounting, volleyball player, babysitter, graphic design, reader of inspirational stories, YouTuber, swim instructor, student council member, juggler, etc.

A Financial Planning Consultant shared a program called "Making Sense of Investment Management." This could have been a boring topic loaded facts. But the consultant was also an avid gardener. She used her gardening skills throughout the entire presentation. She compared investments to plants in the garden. With proper care, the garden produces large, healthy plants that bear seeds like interest. This analogy was easy to understand and interesting. She also had beautiful pictures of healthy plants. This unique twist also simplified a complex subject. She properly used her credibility resources.

Your Credibility Source List might give you important stories, ideas and experiences to include in your presentation.

Credibility Source List

_____

_____

_____

_____

_____

_____

_____

_____

_____

_____

_____

_____

_____

_____

_____

_____

> "Life should be a continuous celebration of who you are and who you are becoming."
> – Cyndee Schweigert

The Topic

The meeting planner might give you a topic to speak about. This eliminates one step in your decision-making process.

If the topic was not assigned to you, you have a lot of choices. Since you already know why you were asked to speak, you know your role. If possible, ask for the program agenda to understand everything happening at the event. If the agenda isn't confirmed, ask the meeting planner to share an event theme if there is one. Also ask what are some topics of other sessions. Learn as much as you can about the event.

Some popular topics include:

Goal setting	Chapter Challenges	Meeting Skills
Team Building	Best Practices	Networking
Officer Responsibilities	Inspiration	Motivation
Social Media Campaigns	Membership Recruitment	Leadership
Public Speaking	Community Outreach	Membership Engagement
Delegation		

My Topic Is

_____

_____

_____

_____

_____

_____

The Objective(s)

You were asked to speak for a reason. The meeting planner believes you have the ability to deliver a good program. After you find your topic, it's time to focus on your purpose. What are your objectives. What is the goal of your presentation?

Do you want the audience to:

- Believe
- Act
- Understand
- Remember
- Support

Your Objectives

Be as specific as you can with your objectives. "Share new chapter membership recruitment programs to help chapters increase their membership by 10%." This is a great goal. It's specific and you can easily share this objective to encourage chapters to increase their membership.

_____

_____

_____

_____

_____

_____

_____

Your objectives are the goals of your presentation. Now you have a solid purpose for your presentation. Even though you haven't even begun writing, it's never too early to start visualizing.

Visualize

Planning doesn't have to be hard work. It can be quite an energizing process. The more you invest in each step, the better it will become. As you plan each step of the presentation, visualize its role and effect on the audience. Clearly imagine the faces of people smiling and nodding in the audience. View the event thru your eyes as if you were actually delivering the presentation. The excellence you create as you visualize will build your confidence and your expectations.

The Close

A presentation is like a race or an archer's target. Crossing the finish line or hitting the bull'seye is an exhilarating feeling. Your job as presenter is to drive the audience to the close – the bull's eye or finish line. Odd as it may seem, your planning starts with the end of your presentation.

The close is your judgment point. The close might be emotional, fact-filled, or a review of what you presented in the opening and the body. Designing the close first helps you keep to the purpose of the presentation.

The Opening

How will you set the stage or get the audience's attention? You know where you want to take the audience – to the close. But first you need to introduce your points so the audience understands your purpose. The opening is the foundation or the building blocks to invite the audience to continue listening. You want to create an Eye Opener opening.

The Introduction is the first segment of the opening. This is where you build your credibility and believability. Create a short introduction that shares your expertise and some friendly things about you. The last thing the introducer should say is "Please help me welcome our [insert your officer title] from [insert your chapter or town], [insert your name]."

The Opening is where you reveal the purpose of your presentation. It's also where you start to create team spirit and fellowship with your audience. You want them on your team to enjoy their time in the presentation. Do something small or large to engage them. This could be sharing fun questions and asking them to respond. This could be a serious, provocative story to grab their attention. This could be a fun word they say when they agree with something. The opening is your opportunity to set the stage and engage your audience to listen to your message.

The Body

The majority of your information is delivered in the body of the presentation. The opening introduces points and your purpose. The body emphasizes and explains the points. And the close repeats the points.

Creating the body is relatively easy because you know where you are starting and ending. You only need to build the path between the two points.

Your tools to build the body are note cards or papers. List a main point you want to share on each card or paper. As you write down more and more ideas, you might need to toss one to the side if it isn't a favorite any more. You're shopping for your best ideas to include in the presentation.

Of course, you can also do this on a digital platform, but there is something magical about physically moving your ideas around.

Mentally and verbally review the points. Consider different sequences. Change the order of the points until you feel comfortable with the flow of ideas. Always remember the purpose and objectives and use the main points to support these. If a main point won't help reach these objectives, don't use it.

"Do more than exist: live.
Do more than touch: feel.
Do more than look: observe.
Do more than read: absorb.
Do more than hear: listen.
Do more than listen: understand.
Do more than think: reflect.
Do more than just talk: say something."
– John Mason

Personal Polish

A presentation is more than simply a string of ideas and words. It's you. Your creative ability to bring the subject to life is vital. Personal polish is the trademark of an excellent presentation.

Personal polish may be a:

* Story
* Joke
* Structured Group Activity

* Question and Answer Period
* Brain Teaser

* Interesting Statistic
* Magic Trick
* Analogy

Remember the managing investments presentation explained as a gardening process. This is an excellent example of an analogy used as personal polish. Any creative thing used to add a unique touch is personal polish. Be cautious not to include too many activities or additions. Remember this is the polish, not the meat of the presentation.

Be courteous if you are presenting an activity or story you learned from some other source as polish; give credit to the source. This recognition creates more credibility and respect for you as a knowledgeable and well-versed presenter.

You may have seen an amazing activity presented in a workshop that you want to use. But before incorporating it into a presentation, ask yourself, "Does adding this help achieve my objectives?" Stories and activities are fun, but they must serve a purpose.

The Natural Delivery

You have built a great presentation. Your purpose and message are clear. But you are not ready to present the information. Why? It isn't natural yet. Even the most talented speakers and actors have nervousness or stage fright before performing. How do you overcome this situation? You don't, but you use it to your advantage.

Stage fright or apprehension is nervous energy. This nervous energy may be the death of your presentation or its life. You make the decision. How well you rehearse and know the information will make the difference. The best remedy for nervousness is to memorize the first two minutes of your program. Regardless of the butterflies, you will be able to deliver. You want to focus your energy on what you are saying and say it well. Nervousness will distract your attention from the message to your uneasiness. Memorizing the first two minutes allows you to channel this energy into your presentation. If you know it, you won't blow it.

The close is your last point of impact. The audience will typically forget about 75% of what you say within 24 hours. The part they will remember is the close. Know it well enough to be extremely dynamic.

Documentation

Congratulations! You have a well-organized, purposeful presentation. It took a lot of your time to create this solid program. Invest a little time to make a permanent record. There is no need to rebuild or rewrite the program if it is done well the first time. Capture the highlights for the future.

Subject: _____

Title: _____

Type of Presentation: Workshop   Keynote   Other

Intended Audience: _____

Objectives: _____

_____

Opening: _____

_____

Body: _____

_____

_____

_____

Close: _____

_____

Materials/Supplies: _____

_____

_____

The Monumental Miscellaneous

Time

If you're asked to speak for 45 minutes, plan a presentation no longer than 40 minutes. Someone will introduce you which takes time. The program might be running a little late. The audience may ask a few questions which take time to answer. You're considered a good presenter if you finish within your time limits. Besides, as an audience member, wouldn't you appreciate finishing a little early?

Topic Flare

Your program will be listed in the program agenda. You've invested a great deal of time building a quality presentation and want people to enjoy it. Delegates want to attend exciting and interesting sessions. Your listing in the schedule is a marketing tool to attract an audience. Make the topic sound exciting.

Pronouns

The shortest route to bomb a presentation is delivering an *"I"* speech. You want to create a bond with the audience. *I, me and, my* don't achieve this objective. Instead, use *you, we, and our*. The audience will respect your attitude implied by your vocabulary and listen more closely.

Rehearse

The best way to improve is to watch yourself. Rehearsing in front of a mirror is good, but digitally capturing your rehearsal is much better. You can critique the file later as a spectator better than the dual role of presenting/critiquing in front of a mirror. To better understand your presentation skills, watch the rehearsal at least three times. The first time, watch your visual image with the sound turned off. Next, turn your back to the screen and listen to your audio message. Last, watch the collective product of your voice and body presenting.

Smile

Need we discuss this? Everyone appreciates your positive smile.

Equipment

Investigate the room before the audience arrives.

- Can everyone see you and your visuals?
- Does the microphone work?
- Is there water and glasses on the tables?
- Is your slide deck ready to start?
- Do you have your notes with you?
- Is the projector framed properly on the screen?

It's easier to make arrangements to correct a situation than make excuses for imperfections.

Involvement

Stage or no stage, you don't have to stay in one place. Move in a natural manner to put the audience at ease. Involve the audience as much as possible. If you know their names, use them. Use comfortable eye contact with everyone.

Difficult Questions and Disagreements

If the audience poses a difficult question, stay calm. If you don't know the answer, tell them you don't, but offer to find the answer for them. Disagreements within the audience might happen. Again, stay calm. Simply state the information you have available. Don't start an argument or use your own emotional responses. It's much more difficult for a member of the audience to argue or doubt the facts than your personal beliefs.

Attention

Everyone has a limited attention span. And it seems attention spans are getting shorter and shorter. You need to keep everyone engaged. Eye contact, visual aids, questions, activities, stories, movement, polling and so much more are all tools to keep attention. When you're building your presentation add personal polish – a story, a joke, questions, group activity – very often. The audience may not know why you are so interesting, but you will.

Evaluation

After you're finished, ask for some anonymous feedback. This could be a small printed card with a few questions. Or it could be a digital poll. Getting feedback can be helpful. Here are a few good options of questions to ask:

1. What's the best thing you heard in this session?
2. What was your favorite part of the session?
3. Rate this session 1 - 5.
   1 = Awful 3 = Average 5 = Awesome
4. The overall presentation was:
   Not Very Enjoyable   Enjoyable   Very Enjoyable
5. The presenter knew the topic:
   Not Very Well   Well   Very Well

Resources

Give the audience resources to review or share with others. This gives your message more impact. Handouts are not necessary, but they are a good supplement for some people. Share links to good information. Preparing a "Capture Sheet" of titles and links to resources as one of your last slides is very helpful. This pic of the capture sheet with their phone gives them a great tool.

Silent Messages

The moment the audience spots you they are judging you. Even before you speak you are telegraphing your enthusiasm for the topic and presentation. Be on your best, attentive behavior.

Lights

You may use some multimedia during your presentation. The lights may need to be dimmed, but always start and finish your presentation with the lights bright. The bright lights will eliminate the audience from nodding off (particularly after lunch) and draw attention to your bright ideas.

Neatness

Ask the meeting planner what most presenters will be wearing. You'll want to dress the same. You do not need a million-dollar wardrobe. Simply invest a few minutes in front of the mirror before presenting. Before you speak, look at yourself. Make certain all of you is sending the right message.

Speaking on Stage

Make Your Message Believable

Know Your Script

Using scripts is so important. Be very familiar with the script, but do NOT memorize your parts. You should show up to your first live rehearsal after having practiced your speaking parts at least TEN times. You must memorize or remember the page number of your speaking parts.

Your Voice is the Message

Say your first three words looking into the audience, not down at the script. This shows your confidence.

Always look into the audience when you –

- say a common phrase (i.e. organization name, the conference theme)
- say peoples' names.
- lead applause

Use very sharp, crisp tones. Try to vary your speed. Always increase your volume at the end of a speaker's introduction. You always want the speaker's name to be the last thing you say. Project your voice as much as possible to sound more enthusiastic. Of course, you should smile because you want to look like you are enjoying yourself.

The Microphone is Your Tool

Adjust the microphone to fit you. You don't want to lean over or stand on your tiptoes. You'll practice this before the general session. Imagine the microphone has a string attached to your chin. You can look around the room but your chin must stay tethered to the microphone.

Physical Appearance is Important

Less is better. Women should wear smaller jewelry. All of the officers should look the same. Maybe have one small pin and a name badge. Make certain you line up before the session to make sure your entire team looks the same. Brushing your face with powder that matches your skin tone – for both men and women – is a good idea. You perspire when you are under the bright lights for a long time. And that gives you a shiny face. The powder will help you look fresh. Dark shoes and socks are the best.

Stand on Stage to Command Attention

Both men and women should stand with their feet square with their shoulders. Your hands should simply be at your side. Never cross or fold your hands in front of you. This stance gives you a firm base where you do not sway and look composed.

Officer Introductions

Always have an enthusiastic smile.

Walk with a purpose using sharp, crisp movements.

Walk confidently with your head up.

Calling the Session to Order

The President should practice rapping the gavel on top of the lectern looking into the audience. This makes you look very polished. The President needs to know these first few sentences. This paragraph sets the tone for the entire conference. It needs to be extremely polished.

Introduction of Someone Coming on Stage

Members who are a part of the organization or are bringing greetings should usually come from backstage. Keynote speakers often come from the audience. The introducer's job is to build as much excitement for this person as possible. The introducer should:

- say this person's name with a "punch" – with more enthusiasm.
- lead applause.
- wait at the lectern for the person to approach the lectern.
- shake the person's hand and guide them to the lectern.

Leading Silent Applause

Leading applause from the microphone is enthusiastic but silent. You should clap away from the microphone and "just above" the podium. Try to look like you are naturally clapping. While you are leading your silent applause you want to look into the audience with an inviting expression for them to also clap.

Giving Awards

When you give plaques or awards you want to hold the plaque with a great deal of respect. The plaque should face the audience but be careful for the glare. You present the plaque to someone by giving it with your left hand and extending your righthand underneath to shake hands with the recipient. It is very appropriate to say something nice or "congratulations" while you are shaking this person's hand.

Controlling the Stage

Of course, you congratulate individuals when you give them an award or plaque. After the plaques have been awarded you are responsible for getting these people off stage. There are many ways to keep the program running smoothly and get people off stage –

- By extending your hand to where you want them to exit, or
- Gently guiding them with your hand in the middle of their back, or
- By saying "congratulations" again and leading the with your eyes or where to exit.

Adjourning the Session

The President usually adjourns the meeting by rapping the gavel. This should be well rehearsed because it is the final impression of the audience. The President should memorize the closing paragraph so it can be said directly to the audience. The President should remain at the lectern after the gavel is rapped until the stage lights are turned off.

"When archers miss their marks,
they turn and look for the fault within
themselves. Failure to hit the bull's-eye
is never the fault of the target.
To improve your aim, improve yourself"
– Gilbert Arnald

Speaking on Stage Checklist

Know Your Script

- Read the script aloud at least ten times before the first rehearsal
- Know the page number of your speaking part

Remember

- There always needs to be something picture-worthy on stage
- Look up when you share common phrases, names, and lead applause
- If something goes wrong, smile and breath
- No one knows your script
- You can adjust the microphone to your height
- To speak to all sections of the audience and the camera lens
- Most people are watching the big screens, so the camera reaches more people

Prepare Your Body

- Drink lots of water
- Eat something nutritious
- Practice deep breathing
- Stretch your body beforehand
- Take a moment to feel grateful

Physical Appearance

- Ties are on correctly
- Pockets emptied
- Few if any pins on jackets
- Shoes are shined/buffed
- Powder on your face

"Give me six hours to chop down a tree and I will spend the first four sharpening the axe."
– Abraham Lincoln

PLUS – DELTA Debriefing Tool

Ground Rules for Successful Debriefing

The Basic Assumption: We believe that everyone participating is intelligent, well-trained, cares about doing their best, and wants to improve.

Discussion during debriefings should remain confidential.

The debriefing must be non-threatening. It is ok to politely disagree, but do not assign blame.

Participants should maintain professional behavior. Be polite, respectful and curious. There should be no interruptions or outside conversations.

Debriefings are a time for critical reflection.

Steps to Leading a Debriefing

Identify and agree on what happened, starting with junior members of the team.

Identify what the team did well.

Ask, "What could we have done differently? Look at any processes or resources that affected the outcome.

Identify lessons learned and the actions that might arise from the process.

Plus **This Went Well!** **Do Again.**	**Delta** **This Needs Improvement.** **Change it.**
• Able to learn parliamentary procedures • Being able to talk to other presenters	• Virtually, we should be able to participate • Unable to network

> "Without reflection, we go blindly on our way, creating more unintended consequences, and failing to achieve anything useful."
> – Margaret Wheatley

Virtual Meetings Mindfulness

Virtual events and meetings will be quite common. Virtual doesn't have to be bad. We are smart humans and we can do amazing things to make the virtual meeting highly interactive and highly engaging. You just need to plan to make it work. There is no such thing as "winging" a virtual event. You create a flow with purpose and connection.

Always remember – Connection always comes before content.

Tips for Leading Virtual Events

Start Strong

- Connect with attendees beforehand to get them excited.
- Encourage people to bring something to share if it's a smaller group.
- Feature "member spotlights" where randomly selected individuals share a 30-second introduction.
- Start the meeting early and encourage people to share answers to fun questions in the chat box. Fun questions could be "What are you looking forward to this month?"
- Encourage attendees to bring their energy. Pose fun generic questions like "You enjoy going to the beach!" Ask them to give a thumbs-up or thumbs-down or jazz hands or spirit fingers to show their reactions.
- Before you start sharing information, make certain you first connect with your audience. Let them feel they are a part of something.

End Strong

- Create interactive pieces throughout the session.
- Use breakout rooms for larger groups to separate and talk about a topic or solve a challenge.
- Use interesting slides.
- Ask for comments to be made in the chat box.
- Create pairs or groups as accountability partners or breakout buddies to follow-up after the meeting.
- Share a Capture Sheet at the end with important resources attendees might want to use later.
- Share a survey or poll to ask for their impression of the meeting and their needs.

Tips for Attending A Virtual Event

- Show up early. If the event starts at 9:00AM, make certain you are digitally connected by 8:57AM.
- Remember you are NOT simply a blob in a box. You have energy to bring to this meeting. Nod your head. Smile. Give a thumbs-up. Give silent applause. Echo positive thoughts in the chat box. Bring and show your energy.
- Make certain you are well lit and your space looks bright.
- Make certain you are well groomed.
- Make certain there is nothing political or offensive in your background.
- Turn on your video. You are at the meeting. People want to see each other.
- Clean up the area where you'll be joining the call.

Introducing Speakers

Introducing a speaker is a big responsibility. You set the tone for the audience and make the speaker feel comfortable. Often introducers don't help either the audience or the speaker. Here are a few simple "do's" and "don'ts" that will help make your next introduction responsibility a successful experience.

DO

- Ask speakers what they would like you to mention in the introduction.

- Pronounce speakers' names and titles correctly.

- Relate speakers' credentials to the audience.

- Make speakers human by mentioning warm facts about them. For example, "Mr. Jones is the father of three children."

- Mention that busy speakers have invested their time to speak to the audience.

DO NOT

- Announce that the speaker is the best the audience will ever hear. This places unnecessary pressure on the speaker and creates enormous expectations in the audience.

- Recite the speaker's entire biography.

- Emphasize a negative. For example – room temperature or a poor microphone.

- Speak for a long time. You are the introducer, not the speaker.

Making Your Message Stick!

(Meeting/Presentation Skills)

Whether you're meeting with five people or 500, you must focus on three items: **Presence, Passion, and People**

Yes, the basics of Speech 101 will always be true. You need to have an introduction, body, and a close. Or said more simply – Tell them what you're going to tell them; Tell them; and Tell them what you told them. Before anyone will give you their attention you've got to look like someone who deserves their attention.

Meeting and presentation skills are hot topics. People are extremely challenged to get attention. Audiences are stressed out and constantly bombarded with stimulus that screams "Look at me!" The days of someone standing up in a meeting and delivering their information to patient eyes and ears are gone.

Meeting skills and presentation skills are closely related. Both are sharing information. The key is how to make the information or message stick.

Presence

Before you begin the meeting or your presentation you have to look like you have something to say. It's that thing called aura or presence or command of attention. Even if you aren't oozing with charisma, you can create a presence.

Own the Space

Before you open your mouth, you need to physically own the space. Far too many people start blabbering as they walk toward the podium or stage. Don't say anything before you've established your presence. Briskly walk to where you'll speak and plant your feet. Your feet should be squarely planted at shoulder width so you physically own the space.

Pause Three Beats

You need to also emotionally own the space before you speak. You should confidently stand looking at several places and faces in the audience. Waiting three long beats (1, 2, 3) while you physically connect with the audience with eye contact further establishes your presence. It may be helpful while you're waiting these three beats to think of some fun phrase to relax yourself, such as – *Oh, this is going to be awesome!* or *There is no place I'd rather be!* or *What a privilege to be here!* or *Let's have some fun!* All of these phrases can help put you in a positive mental place and make you smile.

The few seconds it takes to own the space and pause three beats seems so miniscule, but this is a small strategy that makes a big impact.

Make An Event

Creating presence also includes the bigger job of making an event. It's making people feel something special is happening. What kind of visuals or decorations are you using? Have you given a conference/meeting trinket/gift? Have you given a small something that will reinforce your message?

One organization once gave all attendees small flashlights with the title of the featured speaker's speech – You Make A Difference! – printed on the side. The point of the inspirational speech is only the person sitting in your chair can choose to make a difference. The houselights were turned down, the speaker turned on her flashlight, and said, "Your choice to make a difference seems so small and each of us has the choice to make a difference. Please choose to make your difference and turn on your light. You Make A Difference!" It was an inexpensive way to make an event and members took home a constant reminder of a special moment.

> **Remember the only difference between ordinary and extraordinary is that little "extra"!**

Passion

The passion is the information, meat or content you're sharing with others. If you believe in the words and what you're trying to accomplish people will feel that passion.

You can tell the effect of your words as you craft your message. If you're simply throwing words together you probably won't be effective. Too often we go to a meeting and people just vomit words on us. That is not passion. Your passion is demonstrated by how you share your message.

Make the words come alive. Is there a fun analogy or metaphor you can use? A Past President of the Association For Career and Technical Education shared her gratitude and respect for educators using a popular national marketing campaign with the word PRICELESS. People knew the campaign and appreciated her sentiments. Find creative ways to peak interest and connect with the audience.

Know Your Information. Maybe you're presenting a new national program. It isn't enough to know the information shared from a press release or briefing sheet. Get on the phone and ask some questions. Be ready to answer questions people ask. You could even include a short video of an organization leader reinforcing your message. People will listen when they see the passion from the presenter.

People

The purpose of your meeting is to share information or inspire an audience. We must plan well and respect the investment of time.

Consider this. If just 50 people show up for your one-hour meeting, 50 hours of life are invested in that meeting. That means more than two days of life are invested in your meeting. Whatever you're trying to accomplish better be done thoughtfully and respectfully if you're investing that much human life in a meeting.

Seating

Lining up chairs in single file rows is a cardinal sin of meetings. If you're sitting in single file rows of chairs and you look straight ahead, you are looking at the back of the head of the person in front of you. Is that what we want people to see? Probably not. Seating is an important meeting principle that is often overlooked. Here are ways to create meeting-friendly seating.

- Stagger the alignment of chairs in each successive row.
- Eliminate the center aisle for larger groups. Instead, create two side aisles.
- Fan or turn the seats at 30-degree angles into the aisle for smaller groups. This is called serpentine seating.
- Tape off the back rows for large meetings. This encourages people to sit in the front as they fill the room. Have someone assigned to remove the tape once the program starts. This allows latecomers to easily find seats and not disturb others.

The purpose of changing the way we use seating is to make it easier for the audience to see the speaker and feel they are a part of a gathering. Comedy clubs are great examples of effective seating. Most comedians are funnier when you see and hear other people laughing. Your meetings should use the same principles. Let others see the speaker and share in the fellowship.

Let People Interact

People's attention spans are typically less than 5 minutes. Depending upon the age of the group, the attention spans can be much smaller. If you're the speaker you better plan for this or you'll lose their attention. You can use endless ways for individuals to interact. For example, have the audience:

- Raise their hands to respond to questions.
- Give a thumbs-up or thumbs-down to some questions.
- Have them point to someone and repeat a phrase. This can be great fun it you reinforce a point by saying, "You heard me say it, but listen to what this amazingly intelligent person near you has to say . . . "

When you involve your audience, you increase the fellowship of the meeting. The energy people feel from others will feed into your program and magnify your success. One caution is – the larger the group, the less you should have them move away from their seat. It's much easier to keep order and/or stop the festivities if they are near their seat.

Making Your Message Stick in big and small presentations and meetings is about paying attention to a lot of details. If you create presence, share with passion, and involve people you will have a very successful presentation. Good luck as you make your message stick!

Advocacy
Your Social Media Voice

Advocacy is not political.

Simply stated – Advocacy is speaking on behalf of something. Or to be an ally.

You have joined a team to serve your organization. You stepped up and said you would do the best job possible. When you said you were part of the team, you became an ambassador and advocate. Your own social media platforms and all of its history have also joined the team. These posts and platforms are not YOUR own.

Remember you are one team in a long line of other teams before you, and hopefully a long line of teams in the future. Your efforts add to or subtract from the legacy of leadership.

Consider the Legacy of Your Voice

Your voice reflects on behalf of your local, your state and the national organization.

Your state chapter might have hundreds, thousands or tens of thousands of members that you represent.
Your voice is a reflection on behalf of all of them.

Your national membership might have tens of thousands or hundreds of thousands of members. Your voice is a reflection on behalf of all of them.

Those alumni of your organization over the decades count in the millions.
Your voice is a reflection on behalf of all of them.

Regardless of your political beliefs, you must always have a voice of respect and integrity on your social media platforms. Everything you post must honor and respect the office YOU have the honor of serving.

Your office is bigger than you. It's a leadership legacy of many decades. You are an ambassador and an advocate.

> "The great use of life is to
> spend it for something
> that will outlast it."
> – William James

> "Please think about your
> legacy because you are
> writing it every day."
> – Gary Vaynerchuk

Finding Your Advocacy Story

Why Your Experience Matters to You?

Advocacy means supporting and promoting something. Advocacy is speaking on behalf of something or being an ally. You are a member and a product of an organization. It might be Career & Technical Education. You enjoy being a member and leader in your Career & Technical Student Organization. You are THE best advocate because your experience is the current product. Sharing your story is what will make the difference for decisions made for years to come.

How do you find your story? It takes a little time, but worth the investment to find. We're going to help one another find our stories. Yours might be very similar to someone else's or absolutely unique. The magic happens when you discover yours. When you share this message with others, they'll see the sparkle of why it matters to you. This is THE message that will make you a great advocate.

Let's get started . . .

You need at least one partner and a cell phone to capture your conversation. You don't need to video the conversation, simply record the audio. You're going to be interviewing one another to extract the highlights and the impact the organization has had on you.

Start asking these questions with the goal of finding how your CTSO (or other organization) has had the biggest impact on your life. When you hear your partner be more energetic or maybe a bit more emotional keep asking questions about that topic. Often when we start to feel a bit more excited or thoughtful we're getting closer to finding our story. Don't feel you have to ask all of these questions. These are just starters.

1. What made you join your CTSO (or other organization)?
2. Have other members of your family or friend group been members?
3. What's your favorite part of being a member?
4. Have you taken on any leadership roles at the local level? Which ones?
5. Have you taken any trips or attended any CTSO conferences? What was that like?
6. What were your highlights of the conference?
7. Have you competed in any competitive events? Which ones?
8. Was this experience easy? What made it challenging? What was surprising?
9. How has your CTSO participation helped or changed you?
10. You have risen to a stage of leadership where others in your CTSO look up to you. What is one piece of advice you would give to a first-year member of your CTSO to help them be successful?

If you want great statistics and facts about CTE benefits here is a good resource. https://www.acteonline.org/about-cte/

Writing Your Advocacy Story

A key component of any advocacy strategy is finding personal stories that demonstrate the importance of the change you seek.

Personal stories:
- lend credibility
- put a human face on a topic
- engage other's emotions and stir compassion
- move people to action

1. Meet Your Audience on Common Ground

Your first statement should be something agreeable for you and your audience/listener. For example: "I agree with you that we need to find ways for students to stay in school and graduate." Or, "Yes, we definitely need to find more ways to engage students in learning." This first statement should be changed to match your advocacy goals with the particular audience or listener.

2. Share Your Personal Story

How has your involvement made a difference to you. Your story can be an event that challenged you; an experience where you failed; an experience that changed you; or anything else that showcases the impact of your involvement. Include details that will help listeners form pictures in their minds. Use action verbs and adjectives to paint the picture of your story. Shape your story to fit your advocacy goals emphasizing what action you want the listeners to take.

3. Keep the Story Brief

Your story should be no more than **one** page. Less is often better. Keep honing and editing your story until it is succinct.

4. Plan Your Next Steps

- How will you engage your audience once they have heard your message?
- Who do you want to target to hear your message?
- Who else needs to hear your advocacy story?

Written Communication Tips

Write with **positive language** by eliminating the words **"no"** and **"not,"** or by balancing negative statements with positive statements. For example:

You cannot attend the conference. (Negative statement)

Since the conference budget was reduced, the funds are not available to pay for the conference registration. (Balanced statement)

Write using a **you viewpoint**. This style makes correspondence more personal. For example:

The membership is the backbone of the association. (Impersonal statement)

You are the backbone of the association. (Personal statement with you viewpoint)

Keep a record of what you send/share. You want to have a record in case you need a reference. Digitally file documents in folders so you have easy access.

Have someone else **proofread** your correspondence. Misspelled words and grammatical errors can destroy your credibility.

Make certain you **correctly spell** all names.

If a note or card has any **errors**, throw it away and get a new note or card. This card is an impression of you.

Try to **be brief** in your message. Give all the information, but keep it simple.

Use **goodwill** by beginning and ending your comments with friendly and positive remarks.

Always **attach files in the order** they are mentioned in the email. Or if it is a hard copy of information, neatly enclose items in the order they are mentioned.

> **"The quality of an individual is reflected in the standards they set for themselves."**
> **– Ray Kroc (founder of McDonald's)**

Two Time Hacks

1. DIN = Do It Now!

Yep, you are procrastinating when you have something on your To-Do list and you keep putting it off. Even though you keep procrastinating, you know you will need to get it done. You might not be giving it attention, but it might be haunting you. That haunting is the nagging feeling of remembering that you have to do something.

This time hack is called DIN which is the acronym of "Do It Now." Din is also defined as: a loud, unpleasant, and prolonged noise. When this To-Do item is lingering and needs your attention, that nagging feeling is the din. It's an unpleasant feeling and prolonged pressure you hear and feel inside.

So face the unpleasant, prolonged pressure you are hearing and feeling. Just **Do It Now!** Once you get it done, you won't be hearing or feeling that pressure of something that needs your attention. It will be off your list!

2. Use A Tomorrow To-do List.

You may have worked really hard all day and are very excited to be finished. Instead of racing out the door to do something else, invest the time to create your "Tomorrow To-Do List." It's a simple process that makes the next morning smooth. Before leaving, write down everything you need to get done tomorrow. This list provides two wonderful benefits.

First, it helps your mind settle. When you put something on the list for the next day, you've identified it. You won't be obsessing about it in the evening or maybe when you're trying to get to sleep.

Second, the next day you won't waste time thinking about what needs to get done. Your list is ready with the to-do's that need your attention first. This saves you time.

> "It is better to look ahead and prepare
> than to look back and regret."
> – Jackie Joyner-Kersee

Visibility

As a leader, you're willing to accept new responsibilities and invite bigger challenges.

Sometimes it's a challenge to find more opportunities to exercise your leadership skills, but you can create your own path from your current involvement. How? Become an initiator and increase your visibility.

Become A Specialist

Are you a specialist in your field? Or are you a jack-of-all-trades, master of none? You are involved in SO many activities. As a leader you need to find activities where you can become a specialist. An employer hires someone because they are the best applicant. Attorneys specialize in litigation, patent or probate law; managers specialize in marketing, finance or personnel. What is your specialty? Find your niche where you excel. Find those areas that you feel passionate about. Become outstanding in an activity or field you enjoy.

Go The Extra Mile

The leader who is willing to invest an extra day to complete a project and do it right will achieve more. Work late if you must. Dedicating the extra time and effort demonstrates your commitment to projects. This additional attention you give to your responsibilities will be noticed. Achievement comes to those who go the extra mile.

Respect Your Own Achievements

When you are recognized for a job well done, say "thank you." When you prepare reports or projects, share your results with others who may benefit. This not only helps others, but also recognizes the work you've done. You're helping yourself and others achieve more. Be proud of your work, but never take credit for something you did not do.

Recognize and Promote Others

Offer praise and constructive criticism often. Become a habitual card or note sender. People appreciate being recognized. With the enormous volume of email, texts and social media feeds, personal cards are a pleasant surprise. A thank you or congratulatory card sends the magical message that you care and value others. Make a special commitment to recognize others.

Capitalize on Involvement

Active participation in professional associations gives you both internal and external visibility. Individuals that share your enthusiasm for a particular field are members of those professional associations. These organizations help keep you current in your field. Don't just join associations – participate. Organizations often have a long membership list, but few active members. Make a difference and get involved. Your dedication to the association will be respected by others.

Be the Spokesperson

Volunteer to be the spokesperson/presenter whenever possible. Many people are apprehensive to speak in front of a group. Put this fear in the back of your mind. Train your butterflies to fly in formation, rather than overcome you and the presentation. What a visible position! The more time people see you presenting wonderful ideas, the more you'll be considered a person who produces good ideas. If you need additional help to improve your presentation skills, join an organization specializing in public speaking or find some great tutorials.

Promote Yourself

There is a myth about promotions. Individuals aren't promoted by others; they promote themselves by growing out of their present situations and into greater responsibilities. Promote yourself by accepting more challenges. Remember that you're always representing your greatest product – yourself. People may not have the opportunity to speak to you, but they learn a lot from your appearance. Do you project an image of responsible, organized leadership? Be yourself, but be neat. The image you project will either invite opportunities, or eliminate them. Promote yourself!

Accept Challenging Tasks

Volunteer for challenging tasks that appear difficult. These tasks may seem and often will require more time to finish. If you truly want to gain visibility and accept greater responsibilities, the extra effort will be worth the rewards. Others will recognize your champion achievements over challenging tasks and you'll grow as a leader in the organization. You'll also be chosen to accept more important challenges in the future.

Offer Alternative Solutions

New ideas for change and improvement are the cornerstones of progress. For every one hundred ideas discussed only one may be chosen, but if it's your idea – it's golden. Submit your ideas in writing to others who can benefit. If you continue to generate new ideas you'll be considered and respected as an innovator. This is an excellent way to gain visibility.

> "I am here for a purpose and that purpose is to grow into a mountain, not to shrink to a grain of sand. Henceforth will I apply all my efforts to become the highest mountain of all and I will strain my potential until it cries for mercy."
> – Og Mandino

May I Present...

Personal Introductions

Introductions are golden opportunities for networking. They may also be situations where you put your foot in your mouth. Remembering a few simple rules of introductions will enhance your professional and personal etiquette skills.

---

1. Members of lower professional rank are introduced <u>to</u> members of higher professional rank.

For example: a colleague is introduced to a boss
a boss is introduced to a client
an officer is introduced to an adviser
a member is introduced to an officer

2. A younger person is introduced <u>to</u> an older person.

To determine who should be introduced to the other person, memorize these rules of introductions. The first is the most important rule and will help you make most of your introductory decisions. If the individuals have the same professional rank, proceed to the second rule. The younger person should be introduced to the older person. If both individuals are about the same age and professional rank, it may not matter who is introduced to whom. In this instance, consider your relationship and the occasion to help make your decision.

Tips for Better Introductions

Use the name that the introduced pair will use in conversation. You may address a friend as Dave, but a young person should address him as Mr. Jones.

If you have been asked to call someone by their informal nickname, don't use it in an introduction. Instead, use the more formal name in the introduction. The newly introduced pair can decide how personal or informal to make the situation.

Wear name badges on the right for easy reading when shaking hands.

Members of your family are usually introduced to others.

Include a phrase identifying the newly introduced individuals. This phrase provides the individuals with more information to begin conversation and ways to remember one another.

For example: ...my sister, Mary.
                  ...our neighbor, Amy Ellingson.
                  David Morales of Widget Corporation.
                  Genevieve Evans, new Sales Manager.

Married couples are introduced using both their first and last names. For example, Bill and Mary Smith.

Stand whenever possible for introductions.

Introductory Statements

Reverend Long, may I present Jane Best.

Dr. Cortez, I'd like you to meet my mother, Ann Hanes.

Uncle Bill, this is my dance partner, Neil Patel.

Shawna Hill, I'd like you to meet Bob Jones.

Introductions are Pleasant

Introductions are friendly encounters. As a courteous introducer, do not command two people to meet. Introductions such as:

Mrs. White – Ms. Jones. Ms. Jones – Mrs. White;

Professor Taki, meet my sister, Maria; or

Matthew Brick shake hands with Ardis Pierre...

are rude and impolite. You have a responsibility as the introducer to create a comfortable situation for both of the newly introduced individuals.

You are Cordially Invited

The Invitation

It is a privilege to be invited to a dinner party or banquet. After the host invites you, return the courtesy. The host has to plan the menu, number to be served and the seating arrangement. Promptly respond to the invitation to ease your host's planning responsibilities.

Be Punctual

To arrive "fashionably late" is rude. Be on time. Plan your arrival anticipating challenges such as bad weather or heavy traffic. If you must be late, telephone the host as soon as possible. Explain that you've been unavoidably detained.

After your arrival, immediately apologize to your host. Don't make your late arrival a grand entrance. You've inconvenienced your host and guests. This isn't something to draw attention. Don't elaborate on the details or the reasons for your tardy arrival. Simply take your seat and be a model guest.

Be Seated

The host has carefully planned the seating arrangement and will announce to the guests when they should be seated. After the announcement, the host will lead the guests to the table. Each guest will patiently wait until the host specifically tells each guest where to sit, unless place cards are used. After being seated there will be time for conversation before the meal is served. Don't let anyone be excluded from conversation. Make a point to talk to both guests on your right and left. It is very uncomfortable to sit at a table and have no one talk to you.

Dinner is Served

When a meal is served to you, it will be offered to you from the left. The serving utensils will accompany each dish. Neatly serve yourself a moderate portion and replace the utensils how you found them. Don't begin eating until everyone is served (unless it is an extremely large table). If you're in doubt when to begin, watch your host.

Dinner is Finished

After the meal is finished, remain seated and enjoy conversation with those around you. When your host stands or makes an announcement of where you're going next, sit quietly and listen to the instructions. After you've been informed of the next activity for the evening, follow the instructions.

Time to Leave

Leaving may be the most difficult part of the evening. It is impolite to abruptly leave after dinner or stay extremely late. If you're unsure when to leave, wait for others to leave first. When you've decided to leave, say goodbye to those near you and thank your host. Don't announce to all of the guests that you're leaving. The host will usually walk you toward the door after they've been thanked. Don't prolong your goodbye at the door. The host has to spend time with all of the guests and be available for others to thank. Simply say goodbye and leave.

The Next Day

Your host spent time and effort entertaining you. Make certain you thank your host in writing. The following day is the best time to send this thank you. Your host will appreciate your thoughtfulness. Immediately sending the thank you informs the host that the evening was important to you.

Table Manners

Table manners are extremely important. You will have many opportunities to demonstrate your skills at the table. A leader is courteous and graceful. The following are guidelines to help you improve your table manners.

DO

- Keep handbags and briefcases out of sight during meals.

- Include all members at the table in conversation.

- Place your napkin in your lap as soon as you are seated.

- Use silverware in the order in which it is placed on the table. This is the "outside in" rule.

- Bring food to your mouth, not your head to the plate.

- Chew with your mouth closed.

- Refrain from talking with your mouth full.

- Keep your elbows close to your sides, not on the table.

- Wait for your food to cool, don't blow on it.

- Ask for replacement of soiled silverware at a restaurant, don't clean it with your napkin or sleeve.

- Leave your soup spoon on the plate or saucer, not in the bowl.

- Lay your napkin to the left of your plate when you are finished.

- Place your soiled knife with the cutting edge toward you after eating.

- Remove pits with your fingers and unobtrusively place them on your plate.

- Break bread, rolls and muffins into small pieces which are individually buttered and eaten.

- Dip your fingers into the finger bowl and dry them on the edge of your napkin.

- Be punctual as a courtesy to everyone.

- Compliment the host for excellent food, but don't complain about poor food and service in a restaurant.

- Pass food to the right.

- Wait until everyone is served before you begin eating.

- Gently blot your mouth with your napkin before drinking.

- Keep your head up and back straight while eating.

- Excuse yourself from the table whenever you must leave.

- Dip the spoon away from you when eating soup.

DO NOT

- Fold your napkin neatly after you finish a meal.

- Make noise clanking silverware against your plate.

- Chew with your mouth open.

- Toss your napkin onto your plate after a meal.

- Drink or talk with food in your mouth.

- Leave a bit of everything on your plate.

- Complain about poor service or food.

- Let everyone know what food you like and disliked.

- Tilt your chair back when you are finished eating.

- Push your plate away when you are finished eating.

- Rest your elbows on the table.

- Begin eating the instant you are served.

- Slurp your soup.

- Use your fingers to push food onto your fork.

- Clean your teeth at the table.

- Spit out unwanted food particles.

- Place soiled silverware on the tablecloth.

- Wave your silverware while talking.

- Use your napkin as a bib.

- Polish spotted silverware at the table.

- Leave your soup spoon in the bowl.

- Initiate conversation when someone obviously has food in their mouth.

- Tap your fingers on the table.

- Blow or wave your hands to cool food.

- Announce that you are going to the restroom as you leave the table.

- Drink from the soup bowl to enjoy the last few drops.

- Shove the entire spoon in your mouth.

- Lick your fingers.

> "Good manners are just a way of showing other people that we have respect for them."
> – Bill Kelly

CHAPTER & TEAM OPERATIONS

Patty Hendrickson™

INSPIRING LEADERS

Team Building!

It's More Than Collecting People

> "There are many objects of great value which cannot be attained by unconnected individuals, but must be attained if at all, by association."
> - Daniel Webster

Yes, teams are needed to get work done. But teams are much more than just groups of individuals. There is a lot of talk about teams as if everyone understands. Let's start at the beginning.

What is a Team?

A team is a group of two or more individuals who are working together to achieve a common goal or outcome. Most effective teams have from six to twelve members. Sounds pretty simple, right? Well, it isn't as simple as it sounds.

There are so many organizations that want to use teams because they think teams will be THE answer. Unfortunately, many organizations are disappointed when teams are formed and performance doesn't immediately improve. One of the reasons for the disappointment is the team isn't set up to succeed. It takes time and energy at the beginning to make teams successful.

Let's take a look at teams – what they are and how you can help build teams. The definition of teamwork shows the importance of the amount of freedom or autonomy of team members to create an effective team:

Teamwork: Joint action by a group of people in which each person subordinates his individual interests and opinions to the unity and efficiency of the group.

52

Here's a continuum of the level of freedom or autonomy for teamwork among three different types of work groups:

Committee   **Team**   **Self-Directed Teams**

Lower Autonomy   **Medium Autonomy**   **Higher Autonomy**

It's important to understand the different levels of freedom or autonomy for these three different work groups. The focus of the team building discussion is on teams that have at least medium freedom/autonomy and ultimately have the power to become an effective team. The beauty of teams is the ability for the process to help individuals discover their own talents/skills as they explore their possibilities. It can be an energizing experience if teams are implemented with care.

Most individuals have experience, both good and bad, serving on committees. To help understand what can go wrong when you are part of a work group, here are some reasons why people dislike serving on committees. Look closely at the pitfalls as you begin to plan for your team's success.

Why People Dislike Serving on Committees

Poor leadership
Assignments are not taken seriously by committee members
There is a lack of focus on the committee's assignment
Recommendations of the committee are often ignored by others
Waste of time
Lack of follow-through by committee members
Domination of one person or clique
Lack of preparation by committee members
No action taken
Personal or hidden agendas of members

Now, here are the reasons why people like serving on effective committees. Look closely at the positives as you begin to plan for your team's success.

Why People Like Serving on Effective Committees

Clear role definition of the committee
Careful time control
Members listen and respect one another
Informal atmosphere that encourages discussion
Good preparation by the chair and members
Members are all qualified and interested
Interruptions are avoided or held to a minimum
Good minutes or records are kept
Committee periodically assesses its own performance
Committee members feel they are given some kind of recognition
The work of the committee is accepted and used

We should learn from people's likes and dislikes. To create effective teams – that means a group of people who really do teamwork and aren't just called a "team" – requires careful planning.

"Chance favors the prepared mind."
– Louis Pasteur

A critical factor to the success or failure of the team is how thoroughly the planning and/or designing of the team is done. This planning/designing should not be a mandate from someone outside the team; it's a process of how the team members actually decide to work together. Here are the eight elements of effective teams.

A Clear Elevating Goal

This is THE most important of the eight elements. Team members must all help create the clear elevating goal or mission for the team. What is the reason for the team's existence? What is the ultimate vision that we should try to achieve in all our activities? The goal or team vision cannot be given or mandated from outside the team. It must be created by team members for team members to understand and commit to their purpose.

A Results-Driven Structure

Team members need to create a structure that will get things done. What will be the basic method for doing work? Will people do individual work and bring it to the team? Will the team discuss all items before action is taken? How will decisions be made? Will we use consensus, a majority vote, or leave some decisions to subgroups that are assigned work? How will we make certain that work gets done? Understanding how work will be done and decisions made lets everyone feel a part of building the team. People need to have confidence in the structure to get things done.

> "Success is turning knowledge
> into positive action."
> – Dorothy Leeds

Necessary Features of Team Structure

Clear Roles and Accountability
- Everyone is accountable all the time

An Effective Communication System
- Information is easily accessible
- Information comes from credible sources
- Opportunities exist for members to raise issues not on the formal agenda
- Methods are used for documenting issues raised and decisions made

Monitoring Individual Performance and Providing Feedback

Fact-Based Judgments

Competent Members

Team members need to have: (1) the necessary technical skills and abilities; and (2) the personal characteristics to achieve excellence while working with others. If some members don't have the technical skills and abilities, the team should make arrangements for training of these members. If some members aren't committed to working with others, this needs to be addressed at the start of the team process. This could be an enormous challenge if someone has a hidden agenda or only a personal motive for being a team member. Team members should also discuss their skill sets. What are their strengths? What projects or assignments have they completed? What is their favorite part of their work? What do they like least?

Unified Commitment

Team members must discuss their own realistic priority level for teamwork. Is this the only team they serve? Are they passionate about this project? Some people may see their assignment as a highly significant assignment and want to devote enormous amounts of time and energy. Others may see it as important, but lower on their priority list. This discussion among team members in the beginning helps everyone understand one another. If challenges start to surface, it's important to know as much about one another as possible.

A Collaborative Climate

Team members should discuss how to create a team atmosphere where everyone is welcome to share. Can anyone put something on the agenda? Is there time at team meetings for individuals to raise concerns? What happens when there are differences in opinion? Will a mediator be needed? How can differences be dealt with to maintain the respect for individual members and the commitment to the team? A collaborative climate involves trust among team members. Trust is a result of involvement and autonomy.

The Importance of Trust

Trust allows team members to stay focused.
Trust promotes more efficient communication and coordination.
Trust improves the quality of collaborative outcomes.
Trust leads to compensating (picking up the slack for each other).

Standards of Excellence

Team members need to share expectations. The team needs to listen to one another discuss important issues like: What are your biggest concerns about this team? If things were working well, what would it look like? If everything went wrong, what would the team do? What does "good" work mean to you? What are ways we can ensure positive outcomes?

External Support and Recognition

The team should decide what they will need as an external support system. Do they want supervisors/advisors involved in the process? How would they like to receive information from others? How will they celebrate their successes and give recognition?

> "New leaders do not make all decisions; rather they remove the obstacles that prevent followers from making effective decisions themselves."
> – Warren Bennis

Principled Leadership

The team leader in an effective team is the key to helping guide the team. Effective team leaders serve more as "coaches" to members. The leader helps members discover what they need by way of resources and also serve as a role model. As coaches, they are instrumental in establishing the team vision, creating change that lets the team flourish, and unleashing talent in others. The team leader's attitude toward achieving the team goal is the key for team success.

Team building is an exciting opportunity for individuals and the organization they serve. Understanding the process will improve the chances for your team's success. Ultimately, your commitment and enthusiasm will help in all areas of your team's growth.

Team Development Stages

Last century, psychologist Bruce Tuckman created the model of team development most people reference to explain the team process. The five stages are all important in creating a high performing team. Use this framework to reflect on how your team is building and flowing thru the stages. The ultimate goal is to reach the 5th Stage of Mourning.

#1 Forming

The team is new and very pleasant. Most team members are excited to start the work and get acquainted.

This stage focuses on the people. You'll probably discuss timelines, ground rules, member's skills and interests, project goals and roles.

#2 Storming

The reality of getting a project finished is realized. The niceties are less important and personalities may start to clash.

This stage is where individuals start to notice differences and some annoyances. This is where conflicts arise. Teams that try to avoid conflict only make it worse. Teams need to recognize conflicts and find resolutions.

#3 Norming

The team starts to find its rhythm. Work is getting accomplished. Team members are starting to see the strengths of others.

This stage is where work is done and team members feel progress being made. They might still be annoyed by some differences, but the admiration of team member's skills is most important.

#4 Performing

The team is feeling confident and energized by the success they are making. Roles have been clearly established and the team is self-directed. Momentum is building to complete the work.

This stage is where the team feels a great sense of pride for how they are functioning and moving forward. They need little supervision. This is the pinnacle of the stages – the stage that all teams try to reach. Members are motivated, confident and trust one another.

#5 Adjourning

The team has completed the project and disbands.

This stage is sometimes called the mourning stage because the team is no longer working together. They completed the project and built a high-functioning team. The joy of working together on something meaningful is missed.

> "Don't overlook the significance of your smallest opportunities for civilized behavior throughout each day. The future has no bigger moments then we experience right now. The world changes for the better with every act of kindness, and for the worse with every act of cruelty. The future is nothing grander than the very next moment, and it arrives solely from the present."
> – Bo Lozoff

The Chapter Assessment

Your Term of Service!!!
But Wait – Where do you start?

First Assess What You Have

Before your officer team starts creating your Program of Work (or Program of Activities), you need to assess the current situation. What did your team inherit as your concerns?

- Are the number of dues paying members going up, going down or maintaining?
- Are your finances strong and growing, stable or decreasing?
- Are the number of chapters increasing, decreasing or just maintaining?
- Are the number of conference participants going up, decreasing, or maintaining?
- What's the participation levels of your social media challenges?

You start by asking, "Where is the organization/chapter right now?" To answer this question, create a SWOT. A SWOT?

> SWOT means: **Strengths**
> **Weaknesses**
> **Opportunities**
> **Threats**

List everything – concerns, attitudes, programs, successes, setbacks – that affect the organization under the headings Strengths, Weaknesses, Opportunities and Threats. After listing all of these items, discuss the list.

Answer these questions:

- How can we solidify the strengths?
- How can we capitalize on the opportunities?
- How can we decrease the weaknesses?
- How an we alleviate the threats?

With the completed SWOT analysis and discussion, you can set goals. What are your goals for each programming area? For example, Programming, Financial, Social, Membership, Service, Marketing

Now you have purposeful direction. You've examined the current situation and are making targeted plans to maximize your strengths and minimize your risks.

Program of Work

Your Program of Work – or some organizations call it a Program of Activities – is your master plan to lead. It is a must for any organization. An association of only 15 members with a program of work has the ability to achieve more than an association of 5,000 without a program of work.

Too often, leaders simply continue the previous year's program of work without examining the current state of affairs. It might be a good option to continue working on plans of the previous year, but only if it is best for the current circumstances.

For example, the leadership may have devoted the last five years to raising funds for an important national project. Last year, the national project was completed. If current leaders continue to devote their efforts to raising money, it's a waste of energy. That challenge was met. They need to focus on what are the current needs.

Your program of work is a comprehensive plan of action. The program of work is your collection of goals and overarching ambitions. It's your guiding to light to drive your objectives. It is a specific itemization of priorities for what needs to be accomplished.

How can you develop a timely and purposeful program of work? These steps will guide you to build a solid program of work?

1. Discuss the importance of the program of work.

Most leadership teams don't have the luxury of meeting every day or even weekly. They need a master plan to drive their energy. The program of work helps them synchronize their efforts. It's a master plan to focus everyone's efforts on common goals.

2. Analyze the current situation.

It is important to understand what the association is doing right and wrong. It's a good idea to do a strengths/weaknesses and opportunities/threats (SWOT) analysis to understand the current situation. It might also be helpful to review past programs or work.

3. Discuss community, state and national concerns.

What are community, state and national concerns? Are there national or state programs that need your support? Is there a new initiative you need to focus? What are the strongest needs of your members?

4. State what you want to achieve.

After analyzing the strengths and weaknesses and discussing community, state and national concerns, you'll discover many items. Take your time to consider all of your possibilities. Write down everything you would like to achieve. After you have a really large list, start discussing and select the most important items. Finally, create goals to achieve these important items. These will become your primary goals. Remember, it is better to do a few things well than attempt many things and achieve very little.

5. Determine sub-goals and/or activities.

Brainstorm for as many ideas as possible to achieve the selected primary goals. Remember, brainstorming is a positive exercise where ideas are not discussed, they are only generated. Volume is the key to brainstorming. More is better. After you have a huge list, discuss each idea. Throughout the discussion, remember the purpose of the ideas and activities is to achieve your primary goals. Select ideas that will give you the most positive results.

6. Establish realistic target times.

When will the goals be achieved? Will it take a few months, an entire year, or several years? As you discuss potential target times, you'll discover potential barriers to achieve the goals. Some goals might rely upon other activities. It's important to establish realistic target times. Is it – the third week of May or at the upcoming State Conference; or at next year's State Conference?

7. Delegate responsibility.

The primary goals might have sub-goals and/or activities. For example, the primary goal to increase the membership by 15% may include activities to be administered by the membership and public relations committees. Someone or some group needs to be accountable. Identify who has ultimate responsibility for each activity or goal.

8. Inform the membership.

Your membership is the lifeblood of your organization. Your leaders need to remember they are members first, but they know much more than some of the members. Leaders need to help everyone understand the goals and activities planned. Members need to know what is expected of them.

Ideally, the program of work should be presented before committees are formed. When members know what is happening, they might want to serve on particular committees. If members get to pick where to spend their energy, they will probably have a higher level of commitment.

After the program of work is presented, ask for feedback. Praise and potential criticism should all be welcomed. The Program of Work is literally a work in progress which we can always make better.

9. Review the program of work.

Regularly review the program of work. It should be a regular topic at executive council meetings. Are you meeting targets? Are you ahead of schedule or are you lagging? You might need to make some adjustments along the way. Keep the program of work a focus and priority to help drive your efforts.

> "Most 'impossible' goals can be met simply by breaking them down into bite size chunks, writing them down, believing them, and then going full speed ahead as if they were routine."
> – Don Lancaster

Creating Your Chapter Calendar

Do you want to have a successful chapter?

Do you want to have involved and excited members?

Of course! The best way to have a successful chapter and involved members is to know what you're doing. **You need a Chapter Calendar!**

Here's how you can create a great chapter calendar after you've set your chapter goals . . .

1. Brainstorm for possible chapter activities.
2. Select activities.
3. Mark important or "firm" dates.
4. Plan tentative activity dates.
5. Present the calendar.

1.   Brainstorm for possible chapter activities.

List as many ideas as possible of potential chapter activities, projects and events. Officers, members and advisers should all offer their help. You won't use all of the ideas you list, but the more options, the stronger your calendar. Think of possible ideas for all areas of your chapter programs – financial, professional, community service, marketing, and social.

2.   Select activities.

Select activities, projects and events you want to use from your huge brainstormed ideas list. Use the chapter goals set by the officer team as your selection guide. If membership recruitment is your primary goal, then first look for activities that will help you recruit and retain members. When you select an activity you want to use, write a short description on a sticky note. After you've reviewed the entire list of possibilities the sticky notes are your potential activities. The sticky notes will help you plan and modify the calendar as you plan.

3.   Mark important or "firm" dates.

Mark all important dates and events on the calendar. For example, school start and end days, holidays, exams, vacation days, sporting events, prom, homecoming, state and national meetings, and association deadlines. These important or "firm" dates generally won't change. Marking these dates first helps you plan a more balanced program and eliminate future conflicts.

4.   Plan tentative activity dates.

The officer team discusses potential activity dates. Place the sticky notes on the date generally agreed upon to hold specific activities. The team should consider the programming balance after all of the sticky notes listing activities are on the calendar. The officer team may need to rearrange some of the tentative dates to create a well-balanced program.

5.   Present the calendar.

The tentative calendar should be presented to the membership, advisory board and administration for approval. Presenting the calendar and asking for approval is an excellent way to get everyone involved and enthusiastic. If there are no objections, the calendar is approved. The approved chapter calendar should be printed and distributed to as many people as possible.

Membership Recruitment

Membership recruitment is the life blood of an organization. Your founding members had a wonderful mission – build an organization where members can find greater opportunities, compete and develop new skills. This was a dream for future generations. The founding members didn't know your specific name; they only hoped future members would continue the mission. The simple fact that you are a part of this enormous collection of people makes you part of the legacy created.

You have chosen to be a part of the association because of the positive programs and leadership development it delivers. Now it's your turn to perpetuate the ideals of the organization.

Membership recruitment must be an important part of your program of work. The specific officer in charge of membership recruitment needs to be one of your strongest members. We need to make recruitment and retention a high priority.

Recruitment activities are often called "membership drives," but recruitment is much bigger than a short window of time. Every time someone sees your logo they are getting an impression of your organization. Every social media post helps people see what you do. Every mention of your activities within the community helps you build your brand. These are all part of the greater recruitment efforts.

Recruitment is also an internal activity. You can do a huge membership drive and get a ton of dues paying members, but the kind of members you develop determines how successful you are as a recruiter. If you recruit 40 people but only 3 people become outstanding members, that might not a great outcome. Membership education and engagement are critical.

Great recruitment happens when –

- New energized members join;
- New members feel they belong;
- New members start to really participate;
- New members fall in love with the organization;
- New members start telling others about their experience;
- New members start bringing their friends to events.

Consider these two very different scenarios:

Scenario #1

Ashley is interested in joining the National Student Organization (NSO). She asked Vinay, a member of NSO, "What do you do in NSO?"

Vinay said, "Oh, it's fun! We have meetings twice a month where everyone has fun. In October we go to Georgetown for a huge conference with people from a lot of other schools. It's great! We have a really big group!" And Vinay quickly walked away to do something else.

Scenario #2

Luis is also interested in joining NSO. He asked his friend Dara, a member of NSO, "What do you do in NSO?"

Dara enthusiastically replied to the question, "Luis, we do a ton of activities. The goal of NSO is to build leadership and workforce skills in its members. We have an officer team of 10 officers and 8 committee chairs. Every member can pick which committee they want to serve. Some of our committees are: financial, social, community service, banquet, membership education, and conferences. Since I joined two years ago, I have served as Program Chair and now I'm running for Vice President. It's a great opportunity to get involved and learn things you don't learn at school. The Leadership Conference is in October in Georgetown. We compete with chapters from others schools in leadership events and activities. It is SO much fun!"

"When I first joined, I was just going to be a part of our local organization. But our adviser asked and encouraged me to become an officer. I've been a committee chair and it was great. You asked me 'what we do?' NSO builds leadership while learning. It's your decision how involved you get, but there is something for everyone. Does that answer your question?"

Luis said, "It certainly does. Wow, you do a lot in NSO."

Dara laughed and said, "If you want more info about NSO, check out our website. I'll let our Membership Chair, Zach know you're interested. He can talk to you about the things that really interest you."

"Thanks Dara. NSO sounds great!" said Luis.

These two scenarios happen all the time. Which individual, Ashley or Luis, do you think will join NSO?

The most important things that made the 2nd scenario so much better are –

- Dara made time to have a conversation
- Dara had a solid understanding of the chapter operations
- Dara asked if she had answered his question
- Dara said she would share his information with someone else
- Dara left a great impression

> "That which we persist in doing becomes easier – not that the nature of the task has changed, but our ability to do has increased."
> – Ralph Waldo Emerson

How to Attend a Meeting

Prepare

Why is the meeting being held?
Why have you been asked to attend?
How can you contribute to its success?
What should you bring?
How can you benefit by attending?

Attend

Get there on time.
Sit as near the front as possible.
Listen and observe carefully.
Clarify the objectives for complete understanding.
Take notes carefully (you may have to report to others).
Contribute by participating in the meeting.
Collect ideas and materials for others.
Meet as many people as possible.
Personally thank the presenters and speakers.

Follow-up

Review and organize notes for reporting.
Follow-up with ideas and contacts made.
Share materials learned from others.
Apply ideas, techniques and methods learned.
Send comments, thank you's and suggestions to others.

"Things turn out the best for the people who make the best of the way things turn out."
– John Wooden

Maintaining Meeting Control

Whether you are the presiding officer or simply presenting an idea, you want to be effective because your ideas are important. You want to maintain control and/or attention. Whisper groups and wandering attention can destroy a meeting. How can you maintain control?

Change the volume of your voice.

- Raising or lowering the volume of your voice attracts attention.

Change your location.

- Standing up might be a great way to make a statement. If the room is big enough, walk around the room to include everyone. Don't forget to use eye contact.

Involve the audience.

- To illustrate your point, ask questions of the audience. Use people's first names to set a friendly tone and involve everyone.

- Use objects or visual aids to demonstrate your point.

- Picking up an object helps gain attention. Use objects as props to help make your points.

Leaders remember that their voice and the audiences' ears aren't the only channels of communication. There are many ways to share your message. Stimulate as many senses of the audience to get and keep them involved. You'll maintain control if you involve the audience because they'll enjoy hearing and watching what you have to say.

> "You gain strength, courage and confidence by every experience in which you really stop to look fear in the face . . . you must do the thing you think you cannot."
> – Eleanor Roosevelt

Parliamentary Procedure

Parliamentary procedure is a tool to protect the rights of members of an assembly and help an assembly make decisions. The origins of parliamentary procedure date back to the English Parliament of the 1200's. Parliamentary procedure was used by the Second Continental Congress to frame the Declaration of Independence. The Constitution of the United States was also created with the help of parliamentary procedure.

With the basic standards or parliamentary law used by the United States House of Representatives as a guide, General Henry M. Robert wrote and published a standard guide for deliberative assemblies to follow. This 176-page guide <u>Pocket Manual of Rules of Order for Deliberative Assemblies</u> was published in 1876. Robert decided to publish a new, more complete guide of parliamentary procedure after receiving hundreds of questioning letters over the thirty-five year period after the first publication. The new guide, <u>Robert's Rules of Order Revised</u>, was published in 1915. Today, yet another edition, <u>Robert's Rules of Order Newly Revised</u>, is the general guide for most deliberative assemblies.

Parliamentary procedure is a tool, not a weapon. Use of its rules should promote a productive environment for conducting business. Robert realized the power of parliamentary procedure, and said these words regarding its use:

While it is important to every person in a free country to know something of parliamentary law, this knowledge should be used only to help, no to hinder business. One who is constantly raising points of order and insisting upon a strict observance of every rule in a peaceable assembly in which most of the members are . . . [unfamiliar with] these rules and customs, makes himself [herself] a nuisance, hinders business, and prejudices people against parliamentary law. Such a person . . . either [does not understand] its real purpose or else willfully misuses his [her] knowledge.

Parliamentary procedure is a skill to be learned and practiced. Learn all you can about parliamentary procedure to make your meetings more productive.

An Agenda = A Meeting Map

The agenda is a tool to create a productive meeting. The agenda is created before the meeting. It helps all officers, members and guests understand what is happening during the meeting. The agenda is also a type of map. It shows what business needs to be discussed and helps individuals stick to the purpose of the meeting.

Parts and Order of a Meeting

Call to Order
Opening Ceremonies (optional)
Roll Call (optional)
Reading and Approval of the Minutes
Treasurer's Report
Officer Reports
Committee Reports
Unfinished Business
New Business
Program (optional)
Announcements
Adjournment

1. **Call to Order**

   The presiding officer or chair states, "The meeting will come to order."

2. **Opening Ceremonies**

3. **Roll Call**

4. **Reading and Approval of the Minutes**

   "The secretary will read the minutes of the last meeting." (reading of the minutes) "Are there any corrections to the minutes?" (pause) "There being no corrections, the minutes will stand approved as read."

5. **Treasurer's Report**

   After the report is presented by the treasurer, the chair asks, "Are there any questions on the treasurer's report?" (pause) "The treasurer's report will be placed on file for audit."

6. **Officer Reports**

   Officers who have reports to make should let the presiding officer know before the meeting to include their report on the agenda. The chair calls upon those officers who have a report by saying, "The chair recognizes Ms. Davis, Vice President, for a report." If the chair is uncertain if an officer has a report, the chair simply asks, "Does the Vice President have a report?"

7. **Committee Reports**

   The presiding officer and committee chairs should inform each other in advance of the meeting as to whether a particular committee will report. For those wishing to do so, the chair simply calls on the committee chairs for their reports in the order in which the committees are listed in the bylaws or in the order of the committees' creation. "The _____ committee will now report."

   A motion arising out of an officer or a committee report is taken up immediately, since the object of the order of business is to give priority to the classes of business in the order listed.

8. Unfinished Business

The presiding officer **does not** ask for unfinished business. All items of unfinished business are a matter of record (postponed from the previous meeting or not reached on the agenda of the last meeting before adjournment); so the chair **automatically** mentions such items without asking. "The motion to purchase a laptop was postponed to this meeting. Is there any further discussion on the motion . . .?" The motion is stated exactly as moved at the previous meeting.

OR, "The consideration of _____ was not reached prior to adjournment of our last meeting." (If a motion was not made at the previous meeting, one must be made at this time.) The chair may prompt this by the phrase, "What is the assembly's wish?"

9. New Business

"Is there any new business?" Members may propose new business. Each proposal must be disposed of before a new one is introduced.

10. Program

This is the portion of the meeting devoted to entertainment, guest speakers, etc.

11. Announcements

Members may announce information to the general assembly after obtaining the floor.

12. Adjournment

How to Introduce a Motion

1.   The floor is obtained.

    A. After the last speaker is finished, rise and address the chair, "President [name]," or "Madame/Mr. President," or "Chairperson [name]."

    B. If it is a large assembly, give your name.

    C. After the chair states your name, you have obtained the floor. You now have the right to speak.

2.   The motion is introduced.

    A. State your motion clearly and in the affirmative. For example, "I move to establish . . .," rather than "I move that we do NOT establish . . ."

    B. If your motion is lengthy, provide the chair with a written copy of the motion.

3.   The motion is seconded.

    A. Usually a second is required, but there are a few exceptions.

    B. Another member will simply say, "I second the motion," or "I second it."

    C. The member who seconds the motion does not have to obtain the floor.

    D. If no one promptly seconds the motion, the chair may say, "Is there a second?" or "Is the motion seconded?"

    E. If there is no second, the motion is lost.

4.   The chair states the motion.

    A. After the motion is seconded the chair must say, "It has been moved and seconded that . ."

    B. Only after the chair states the motion can debate or voting occur.

    C. The motion may be withdrawn by the mover before, but not after it has been stated by the chair.

5.   The chair calls for debate.

    A. If the question (motion) is debatable or amendable, the chair immediately asks, "Are you ready for the question?" or "Is there any discussion on the motion?"

    B. If the question (motion) is not debatable or amendable, a vote on the question immediately follows the stating of the question.

6.   The motion is debated.

A. The mover of the motion is allowed to speak first.
B. All remarks (debate) must be pertinent to the immediately pending question.
C. All remarks must be addressed through the chair; not to or at other members.
D. Members must properly obtain the floor to debate.
E. A member may speak twice on the same motion on the same day, unless another member who has not debated desires the floor.
F. Movers of a motion may not speak against their own motion, but may vote against it.
G. Members should avoid using the names of other members during debate.

7.   The question is put.

A. After debate appears to have ended, the chair asks again, "Are you ready for the question?"
B. If no one rises, the chair proceeds to put the question – to take the vote. The chair states, "It is moved and seconded that . . . Those in favor of the motion will rise. [pause for the count of members standing] Be seated. Those opposed will rise. [pause for the count of members standing] Be seated."

8.   The vote is announced.

A. The announcement of the vote is a necessary part of putting the question.
B. The chair announces the vote by saying, "The aye's have it," or "The affirmative has it and the motion is adopted," or "The noes have it and the motion is lost," or "The negative has it and the motion is lost."

General Classifications of Motions

Main or Principal Motions

- Are used to bring before the assembly, for its consideration, any particular subject.
- Take precedence of no other motion.

Subsidiary Motions

- Are applied to other motions for the purpose of most appropriately disposing of them.
- Are listed in order of precedence. When one is immediately pending every motion above it is in order, and every motion below it is out of order.

  1. Lay on the table
  2. Previous question
  3. Limit or extend limits of debate
  4. Postpone to a certain time (or indefinitely)
  5. Commit or refer
  6. Amend
  7. Postpone indefinitely

Privileged Motions

- Do not relate to the pending motion, but are so important that they take precedence over all other questions.
- Are generally debatable.

Are listed in order of precedence. When one is immediately pending every other motion above it is in order, and every motion below it is out of order.

  1. Fix the time to which to adjourn
  2. Adjourn
  3. Recess
  4. Raise a question of privilege
  5. Call for the orders of the day

Incidental Motions

Arise out of another pending question and must be decided before the question from which they arise; or incidental motions are incidental to a question that has just been pending and must be decided before any other business is discussed.

- Yield to privilege motions and usually to the motion to lay on the table.
- Are generally debatable.
- Do not have a rank of precedence.

  - Point of order
  - Appeal
  - Suspend the rules
  - Objection to the consideration of a question
  - Division of a question
  - Consideration of a paragraph
  - Division of the assembly
  - Motions relating to methods of voting
  - Motions relating to nominations
  - Requests and inquiries

"The challenge of leadership is to be strong, but not rude; be kind, but not weak; be bold, but not bully; be thoughtful, but not lazy; be humble, but not timid; be proud, but not arrogant; have humor, but without folly."
– Jim Rohn

Engagement

Building an Organization Where People Want to Be!

Are you sometimes frustrated by

> the lack of commitment from some people?
> dwindling enthusiasm for projects?
> a lack of attendance?
> apathy?

This may be the perfect time for reflection. If you're investing time and energy in your organization, you want a return on that investment.

Your organization is more than just a collection of people. It's a mosaic of relationships, interests and energy. You can make your organization so much better by focusing on engaging your members.

A word of caution. If you're not committed to investing the time to build an environment of active involvement, do not read further. These wonderful tidbits or strategies to build your organization take time. And it takes your energy to start the process. If you're willing to commit the time, the payoff is enormous. If you're ready to make a positive difference to engage your members, here are major points to help you make it work.

Membership education/orientation is everyone's responsibility

The days of coming to a meeting and having one person "tell you the ropes" is over. People need to feel connected to as many people as possible from the moment they join. The benefits of having several people welcome them and explain ways to be involved are enormous. We don't all equally get along or "click" with others. If several people are orientating us, the chance that we will "click" with one of them is much greater. Also, the more faces and conversations people experience with members, the greater their comfort. These are the connections – the sparks of excitement – that will help keep these members wanting more.

Fellowship is everyone's responsibility

When we join organizations – whether as a volunteer or employee – the individuals we work with become part of our lives. Whether you are working on a personal or professional project, it is YOU that is working. You can't turn off parts of your life. We need to build as many bridges between people as possible. There must be time for fun and feeling that you are working with someone to make a difference.

> "Do not wait for leaders; do it alone, person to person."
> – Mother Theresa

Recognition is everyone's responsibility

Whether it is a tiny task or a monumental project completed, everyone deserves recognition for their work. Often, we get so busy doing that we forget to value what we've done. The recognition system shouldn't be given to a committee. Instead, make recognition and praise the norm in your organization. Simply start the process. Whether it is small notes, announcements, social media posts, a simple mention of the person's work in front of others, or anything other creative way – just start bragging about people and what they accomplish. Being recognized for what we do makes us feel good. The amazing explosion of good feelings and appreciation is one of the keys to keep our members coming back for more.

Visibility is everyone's responsibility

Members need to feel a part of the big picture. A simple way to get great visibility for our organization is to wear our organizational pride. Whether it's shirts, hats, jackets, stickers or anything else, we can get great visibility wearing or carrying our logo. This is also an internal retention tool. People like to belong to something they can rally around. The more name and logo items members have, the more times they are reminded of the organization.

Participation is everyone's responsibility

Have you ever been part of a group where the leaders or bosses were great at telling others what to do, but didn't do any of the work themselves? It's a frustrating situation. If you are an elected or selected leader, consider your privilege of serving as a type of supportive person. Your election actually puts you deeper in the trenches when a project needs to be done. Think how inspiring it is when you see people working extremely hard regardless of their title. This is truly powerful leadership. It is servant leadership. If you're an elected leader, this should be your goal.

> **"Integrate what you believe in every single area of your life. Take your heart to work and ask the most and best of everybody else too."**
> **– Meryl Streep**

These five strategies are not intended to be told to members. Instead, they should be used to inspire our leaders. The only person we have complete control over is ourselves. Ask yourself these questions and respond as honestly as possible –

Have I made a point to help as many people as possible meet and work together?
Have I relentlessly tried to include as many people as possible in the organization?
Have I celebrated or appreciated all of the work people do for the organization?
Have I found ways to increase the organization's visibility?
Have I served as a member first and officer second in a way that inspires others?

Engagement takes time, but the payoff is huge. Engagement has to start somewhere. Why not let it start with you?

Empower Others to Recommit

Officers Important Role

Officer teams always experience a season of transition. Leadership teams end their terms of service while others prepare to jump into their new roles. It's an emotional time. As a mentor (and stabilizer) you have such a valuable role during this transition.

You've heard these common phrases –

"I've put in my time as an officer. I can't wait to turn over this office."
"I love this office and don't want to give it up."

Both situations probably sound familiar and both deserve care to ease the situation. Here's a helpful suggestion or model to lead your leadership team and organization through a healthy transition. The number one objective is:

Recommit to the Big Picture

Whether the leadership team has one month of one semester remaining to serve, this is a critical time to refocus. Most teams experience the magical realization that they can't do it all in their short term of service. The process of servant leadership also includes realizing what can be done and what should be done. Accomplishing the lofty aspirations and goals from the start of their year of service may seem nearly impossible. This is often a source of defeat for many leadership teams.

> **"I think that being able to communicate with people is power. One of my main goals on the planet is to encourage people to empower themselves."**
> **– Oprah Winfrey**

As a mentor, you play a crucial role in affirming the officers' can-do attitude and keeping the team focused. You can make a huge difference by asking the leadership team a few simple questions. Your discussion will reveal where and how you should invest your energy for the biggest impact.

1. What have we accomplished so far?
2. Does everyone know we have accomplished these things?
3. What have been our biggest challenges?
4. What have we done to deal with some of these challenges?
5. What is THE most important thing for us to accomplish?

Answering these questions can help recommit the leadership team, affirm the positive things they've accomplished and focus their energy on the Big Picture. Empowering others is what you do best!

No Problem!

It's A Challenge

Leaders continuously face situations that require action. The actual situation isn't desirable. A change is needed. Leaders face these situations and turn what some may call a problem into a challenge. How can you identify a problem and confront the challenge?

Identify the Problem

- Introduce the situation
- Describe the situation clearly
- Emphasize the seriousness and importance of the problem
- Arouse a desire to do something about the problem
- Leave no doubt as to the need for the meeting
- Don't suggest or imply any solution
- Get the problem identified clearly by everyone
- Make it clear that it is the challenge of the membership

After identifying a situation that deviates from the desired situation – a **problem** – it's now a **challenge**.

Explore the Challenge

- Ask the group to expand on present conditions or present practices
- Explore for additional evidence of seriousness or need for attention
- Probe for causes and effects
- Explore related or modified angles
- Identify what course to take to improve, alleviate or change
- Identify cautions or difficulties that must be met

Extract Possible Solutions

- Invite solutions, what MIGHT work
- Ask contributors to support their ideas
- Encourage others to question or challenge
- Accept and record all contributions on a board
- Help them think broadly

Decide the Best Course of Action

- Concentrate on evaluation of possible solutions
- Be alert to majority agreement
- Ask for votes of consensus on important elements if necessary
- The key phrase to include: Are you satisfied that this is the best solution or course of action; that it effectively solves the challenge; that it is possible and practical?
- Conclude with assignments and time schedules

> "Do the best you can until you know better. Than when you know better, do better."
> – Maya Angelou

Conflict!

Conflict is generally considered bad. Visions of heated arguments and negative emotions come to mind. But group conflict can also be a positive factor. Conflict occurs when group members have different attitudes or perceptions about a subject. A state committee of representatives from both metropolitan and rural areas is likely to have a wide range of attitudes because of the individuals and areas represented. When each group member is aware of the different life experiences in a group, the group will be able to reach a better and more representative solution. The key is how conflict is handled.

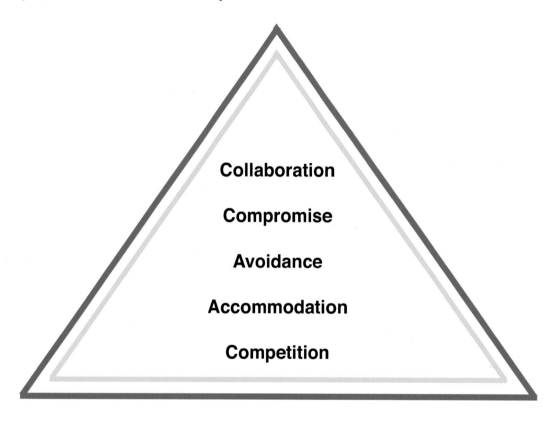

Collaboration

Compromise

Avoidance

Accommodation

Competition

The conflict pyramid shows five ways to handle conflict. The least effective way to handle conflict is the competition method which is at the base of the pyramid. Successful leaders use collaboration at the top of the pyramid because it combines the members' group and personal needs. Each tier of the pyramid has specific characteristics which show the effectiveness of each method of handling conflict.

Competition

Competition is the least effective method of handling conflict. It is a very harmful method which intimidates or bullies members to agree.

- Individuals are not separated from the behavior surrounding the conflict.

- Individuals blame, accuse or label one another. Comments such as *"You are bull-headed!"* or *"Is this another idea of yours about..."* are often used.

- Definitive words such as *should, must* or *will have to* are included in the conversation.

- Rather than emphasizing the cohesiveness of the group, "you" language which separates the individual from the group is used to dominate group discussions.

- Individuals attempt to dominate one another by nonverbally invading one another's personal space.

- Individuals become engrossed in the conflict. They are unable to separate themselves from the situation. As a result, emotional and sarcastic language is common.

Accommodation

Although accommodation does lead to agreement, the agreement does not represent the group. This is only surface agreement often found in groups with a great deal of internal politics.

- Members do not reveal their own needs, perceptions or feelings to others. It may be too big of a political risk.

- The verbal exchange in an accommodating situation is typically repetitive and monotone.

- Individuals have disagreements to the present situation, but have decided to simply "go along" with the group. This is an uncomfortable feeling for some individuals. Their body language is indirect, looking down or away from the group. This nonverbal cue shows that the individual is not comfortable with the group's decision.

Avoidance

Avoidance is similar to accommodation, but the individual does not agree to simply "go along" with the group.

- Individuals avoid facing the group. Members may look away, fidget or completely turn their bodies away from the group. This is an attempt to separate themselves from the situation.

- Individuals neither reveal their own feelings or needs, nor verbally agree with the group.

- Members quickly change the subject when they are asked to provide feedback. They may also rephrase part of the discussion to make it more closely represent what they want.

Compromise

Compromise is an effective method of handling conflict, but it does not satisfy every person. Members' group concerns are met, but not their underlying personal needs.

- Good verbal and nonverbal communication is used. Members verbally speak in team or negotiation talk. Phrases such as *Let's compromise*, or *Let's make a deal*, or *Give and take* are common. Members are comfortable in this situation and use direct body language.

- Members recognize and discuss each other's surface needs.

- Although members discuss the group surface needs, the underlying needs and concerns of the individual members are not shared.

> **"Seek First to Understand,
> Second to Be Understood."
> – Stephen Covey**

Collaboration

This is the most satisfying and effective method of handling conflict.

- Members are not intimidated by one another. Many statements include *I think* or *I believe*.

- Individuals respectfully listen to one another with an open mind. Members separate the challenge or conflict of the group from the individual group members.

- Members are encouraged to generate potential solutions. Positions are not taken. The meeting is an open forum for the exchange of ideas and information.

- Most importantly, members share information about themselves, their thoughts, feelings and past experiences. Individuals are not afraid to put themselves in a vulnerable situation because the group's enthusiasm for team success is most important.

The Five Methods of Handling Conflict

– Competition, Accommodation, Avoidance, Compromise and Collaboration –

Are described as they occur in groups. The same methods are found in personal conflict. Using collaboration requires practice and a keen awareness of how to build the team or success spirit. In order to collaborate, individuals must value their own contributions and know they will be appreciated.

Consider the conflicts you've experienced and how they were resolved. Too often people first try to give advice to solve conflicts. As a leader, try to help the team find a good solution by valuing everyone's input.

Conflict Resolution Strategies

Conflict is not necessarily negative. It is simply a situation. How we mange conflict can be positive or negative. The diplomatic leader understands the important difference between conflict and conflict management and tries to positively manage conflict.

There are no universal rules for dealing with conflict, but there are techniques to help you manage conflict. Understanding these basic strategies can help you manage or even prevent a negative confrontation.

Learn to Wait

If a situation is extremely emotional, waiting may be the answer. Time is a wonderful cure for bruised egos and hot tempers. You'll be much more productive after emotions have calmed.

Use Silence

Silence is a masterful tool which can be uncomfortable. If you want more information from others, remaining silent may urge them to continue talking. Silence is a void which most people feel a need to fill. Use silence to your advantage.

Don't be Afraid to Say, "I Don't Know."

You may be asked a question you can't answer. Simply say "I don't know," but let others know you'll be happy to find information for them.

Size Up the Situation

Before making a firm statement, size up the situation. It may be advantageous to assess the situation before saying something you'll regret.

Be Yourself

Sincerity demonstrates your commitment to the situation. People will be more open to your suggestions if they know you're honest.

Listen Aggressively

Listen aggressively to verbal and nonverbal language. You'll be amazed how much information you learn by listening. You may be able to find a solution to satisfy more people.

Evaluate a Recent Conflict

Evaluate a recent conflict you experienced using the methods of handling conflict pyramid as a reference. Write the details of what actually occurred. Write them as a spectator would report the facts of the incident.

1. What is/was your relationship with the individual with whom you had the conflict?

_____

_____

_____

_____

_____

2. How do you feel about this person? What is your general impression of this person?

_____

_____

_____

_____

_____

3. What was the cause of the conflict?

   (Explain what the other individual actually did, not how it made you feel.)

_____

_____

_____

_____

4. What was your reaction to this cause of conflict?

   (Explain how the behavior made you feel.)

   _____

   _____

   _____

   _____

5. What did you want to accomplish from the conflict?

   _____

   _____

   _____

   _____

6. What was your behavior in response to the conflict? (What did you actually do and say?)

   _____

   _____

   _____

   _____

7. What was the result, both short and long term, of the conflict?

   _____

   _____

   _____

   _____

8. What method of handling conflict was used?

   _____

   _____

   _____

TEAM
REFLECTIONS

Patty Hendrickson™

INSPIRING LEADERS

Team Expectations

Setting Yourself Up for Successes

Forming is the first stage of team development. Team members are very polite and excited to be a part of them team. Use this time of enthusiasm for the team to learn about one another. This could be a casual conversation over a meal or a large planned agenda item on a team retreat.

Here are some excellent questions to ask all team members so we start to learn their tendencies.

1. What social media platforms are you on?_____

2. What social media platforms are you most active on? _____

3. What time of day do you usually get organization work done? _____

_____

4. Do you prefer to be contacted by a call, email, text or something else?_____

_____

5. What days are you most busy? _____

6. Do you have a job? What days/times do you work?_____

_____

7. What time of day is the best to reach out to you if I need an answer fast? _____

_____

8. Do you tend to immediately respond? Or do you take your time to think about something for a while?

_____

_____

To Deepen the Conversation

Please share a negative team experience you had. What made that experience negative and what did you learn from this less than wonderful experience? _____

Vraj - breakout room   Zithi - water polo   Gaurika - Work /manager problem

Raeya - Biology group   Piya - Dance team / didn't show up to practice

Please describe someone that you've worked with that you really admired. What did they do to leave a legacy with team members and help people perform better? _____

_____

_____

Please describe your "awesome sauce." What gifts and talents do you bring to the team? Please share an experience where you helped others be successful because of these gifts and talents. _____ Vraj - Computer programming   Rithi - leadership & organization

Shrp - do whatever   Gaurika - problem solving   Piya - approachable   Raeya - approachable

Rosie? Patience

Please describe your biggest hopes for the team. What will have happened during your term of service that will make you feel your team was successful when you're finished?

_____

_____

_____

> ## "Let's focus on the right things to get traction, momentum and results."
> ## – Patty Hendrickson

What's Happening in Your Team?

A leader identifies the strengths and shortcomings of many situations. Team dynamics is the term used to describe what is happening within a team. Evaluating the team dynamics is important to help the team be successful. Consider what has happened within your team. Examine each person's participation as well as your own. Be as specific as possible.

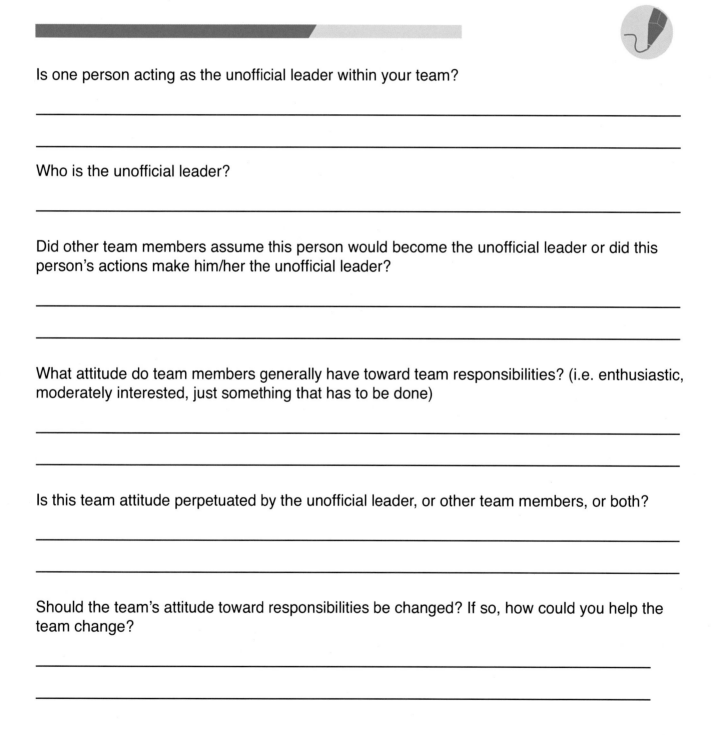

Is one person acting as the unofficial leader within your team?

_____

_____

Who is the unofficial leader?

_____

Did other team members assume this person would become the unofficial leader or did this person's actions make him/her the unofficial leader?

_____

_____

What attitude do team members generally have toward team responsibilities? (i.e. enthusiastic, moderately interested, just something that has to be done)

_____

_____

Is this team attitude perpetuated by the unofficial leader, or other team members, or both?

_____

_____

Should the team's attitude toward responsibilities be changed? If so, how could you help the team change?

_____

_____

Is there a team member who you consider is not included in the team? If so, who is it?

_____

_____

What can you do to include the member?

_____

_____

Are you truly contributing your best to accomplish the team's responsibilities? If not, how can you contribute more?

_____

_____

Is there a particular moment when you were not very proud of your team? If so, when and why?

_____

_____

Is there a particular member when you were very proud of your team? If so, when and why?

_____

_____

Should you continue to be a member of the team?

_____

_____

Do you have other general concerns about your team?

_____

_____

The Classic Jar Story

A lecturer was speaking to a group of competitive and high-achieving people. He placed a wide-mouth gallon jar on the table in front of him. Next to the jar was a collection of fist-sized rocks. He carefully filled the jar with the big rocks, until he could fit no more.

He asked the group, "Is the jar full?"

Everyone replied, "Yes."

He then pulled a large bowl of gravel from under the table and proceeded to pour the gravel into the jar. The gravel fit into the spaces between the rocks. He again asked, "Is the jar full?"

"Probably not," replied the group.

He reached for another bowl, this one filled with sand. He dumped the sand into the jar. The sand filled the spaces not taken by the rocks and the gravel. Once more, he asked, "Is the jar full?"

"No," everyone replied.

Finally, he reached for a pitcher of water and poured water into the jar until it was filled to the top. The time management guru looked at the group and asked, "What is the point of my story?"

One man answered, "That no matter how full your schedule is, you can always fit one more thing into it."

"NO!" responded the lecturer.

The point of the illustration is, "If you don't put the big rocks in first, you'll never get them in at all!"

Individual Jar Story Reflections

1. What are your big rocks – your priorities?

_____

_____

_____

2. What is your gravel – those things that are second in importance?

_____

_____

_____

3. Is it sometimes difficult/hard to keep your focus/energy on the big rocks?

_____

_____

_____

4. If others looked at your "jar" of priorities, what do you think they would identify as your priorities or big rocks?

_____

_____

_____

5. What helps you refocus on your priorities?

_____

_____

_____

6. Who in your life helps you focus or refocus on your priorities?

_____

_____

_____

7. While reading the story/illustration and reflecting on these questions, did anything stand out for you? Did you have an "aha" moment?

_____

_____

_____

Team Jar Story Reflections

1. What are your team's "big rocks" – your priorities?

_____

_____

_____

2. Is it sometimes challenging to keep the team's focus/energy on the big rocks?

_____

_____

_____

3. If others looked at your team's "jar" of priorities, what do you think they would identify as your priorities?

_____

_____

_____

4. What helps the team refocus on priorities?

_____

_____

_____

5. What can the team do to stay focused on these priorities?

_____

_____

_____

6. Do you think this is important?

_____

_____

_____

7. What is your "take-away" or "aha" from this exercise/story?

_____

_____

_____

8. Is there a ritual or habit or practice you could establish to help you stay focused on team priorities?

_____

_____

_____

A Lesson for George and the Jar of Peanuts

A glass jar half full of peanuts stood on a table.

George, who loved peanuts, saw it. He climbed up on the table and thrust his hand into the jar, grasping a whole handful of peanuts. He tried to pull his hand out, but the mouth of the jar was too narrow for his fist.

He pulled and pulled and became very angry at the jar, but it was of no use.

At last he began to scream and cry. His mother hurried into the room to find out what was the matter with him.

"What's wrong George?" she asked.

"This jar will not let me have this handful of peanuts," cried George.

His mother laughed when she saw why his hand was stuck in the jar.

"Must you have so many peanuts at one time?" she asked. "Try taking out a few at a time."

George did as his mother suggested, and found that he could easily get the peanuts out of the jar.

"Now George, next time you get into trouble, stop and think of a way out instead of screaming," said his mother.

Yes, it is a clever story, but what does the story tell you?

What are the learning points?

What advice can you extract to use in your own life?

What learning points would be helpful to remember for your responsibilities?

Lessons from Geese

As each goose flaps its wings, it creates an "uplift" for the bird following. By flying in a V formation, the whole flock adds 71% more flying range than if each bird flew alone.

> **Lesson:** People who share a common direction and sense of community can get where they are going quicker and easier because they are traveling on the thrust of one another.

Whenever a goose falls out of formation, it suddenly feels the drag and resistance of trying to fly alone, and quickly gets back into formation to take advantage of the "lifting power" of the bird immediately in front.

> **Lesson:** If we have as much sense as a goose, we will stay in formation with those who are headed where we want to go.

When the lead goose gets tired, it rotates back into formation and another goose flies at the point position.

> **Lesson:** It pays to take turns doing the hard tasks and sharing leadership – with people, as with geese, interdependent with each other.

The geese in formation honk from behind to encourage those up front to keep up their speed.

> **Lesson:** We need to make sure our honking from behind is encouraging – not something less than helpful.

When a goose gets sick or wounded or shot down, two geese drop out of formation and follow it down to help and protect him. They stay with the goose until it is either able to fly again or dies. Then they launch out on their own with another formation or catch up with the flock.

> **Lesson:** If we have as much sense as geese, we'll stand by each other.

SELF REFLECTIONS

Patty Hendrickson™

INSPIRING LEADERS

Personal Goal Setting
or
What the Heck am I Going to do?

You're often asked questions such as…

- What are your goals?
- What do you plan to accomplish?

These are big questions to answers. It takes an investment of time and energy to create goals.

Some people invest one day to create their personal goals; others invest a week or more. Investing your time, questioning yourself and identifying the things you want help you create more reflective and well-researched goals. Individuals who have specific, written goals are usually more focused or seem to have more momentum.

This step-by-step exercise will help you create and achieve meaningful goals.

> "Without goals, and plans to reach them,
> you are like a ship
> that has set sail with no destination."
> – Dr. Fitzhugh Dodson

What are goals? And why bother having goals?

A goal in the simplest definition is an end that one strives to attain. Goals are targets to work toward. Goals are like distant places or states. By focusing on these goals we direct our energy. If we know where we want to move towards – the goal – we can choose the types of activities or challenges we accept. Goals help us direct our energy and select the activities or responsibilities to reach those distant targets.

This step-by-step goal exercise has four broad steps to help you establish your goals.

1. Examine the present

Goal setting is an exercise of planning for the future. Your goals become your targets. Before writing down everything you want to achieve and creating goals (the things to happen in the future) we first have to learn as much as possible about ourselves (the current situation or what is happening now). We need to identify where we are now and what is most important to us.

We first have to answer some questions about who we are and what we want. What are our values? What things do we value most in our lives? For example: having a secure family life, having financial security, living on a clean and healthy planet, having the freedom to travel, having the freedom to achieve, being a role model, having a healthy and fit body, etc.

A value is defined as: *that which is desirable or worthy of esteem for its own sake; thing or quality having intrinsic worth.*

Creating your list of values is the first step. These are the parts of your life that you need or desire to feel secure. These are the items you find most rewarding.

These Things I Value . . .

_____

_____

_____

_____

_____

_____

_____

_____

The list of values helps you see your priorities. These things are important to you. As you create your goals you need to remember these values to help set goals that will bring or maintain balance in your life.

The next step in examining the present is to investigate what is happening in your life, both internally and externally. This is simply a listing of positives and negatives (or assets = positives; obstacles = negatives). Some of these items you have control over; others you don't. Identifying your current situation helps put you in the best spot to create goals to lead you where you want to go.

Assets are positive situations in your life. For example: a rewarding relationship, a new responsibility, a secure family life, a healthy body, an educational opportunity, etc.

Obstacles are negative situations in your life. For example: a sick relative, the loss of employment, personal illness, the frustration of not fulfilling a commitment, a broken relationship, a death, lack of financial resources, etc.

List as many assets and obstacles in your life as possible. This may take more time than you realize. Many things in our lives we assume as part of your normal routines. We may not recognize the individual circumstances or parts of these routines. Closely evaluate your daily activities. This may also be a little painful, but it is important to recognize as much as possible. Try to look beyond the surface and identify the assets and obstacles in all parts of your life.

What's Happening in My Life?

Assets   *Obstacles*

_____

_____

_____

_____

_____

_____

_____

_____

2. Look to the future

We've identified where we are now. The second step is to look to the future. Where do we want to go?

Start by creating your Dream List. This list is everything you would like to DO, HAVE or FEEL. There are no limits. List items that are ridiculous as well as practical. Write down anything you can imagine that you might possibly want to achieve. Reality is not considered important at this point. Your Dream List should be enormous. The quantity of items you would like to DO, HAVE or FEEL is important

My Dream List

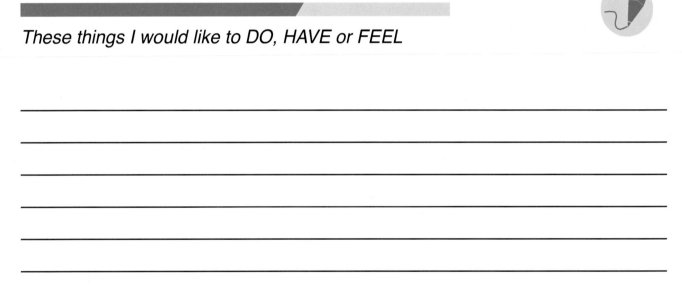

These things I would like to DO, HAVE or FEEL

_____

_____

_____

_____

_____

_____

Your long Dream List is the start of creating your goals. At this point you may want to put aside your Dream List for awhile and look at it again in a few hours or a few days. Take a mental break and return to the list with a fresh attitude.

-Take a Break-

Look at your Dream List once again. Carefully read each item you listed. (It's okay to laugh at some of the outrageous items.) After you've read each item, review the list again. This time eliminate those obviously outrageous items. The objective of eliminating items is to shrink the list or narrow your focus.

Whether you've narrowed the list to have four, three, two or one remaining item(s) doesn't matter. Your objective is to narrow your focus to the bigger items. Some of the items you list may be steps in the process of achieving other items listed. Select the items that are most important to you.

For the remainder of this goal setting exercise, you'll focus on only one of the items listed on your Dream List. You'll use the same process to develop all other items on the Dream List into goals.

Select only one of the items remaining on your Dream List. Write this item below.

_____

_____

The next step is to create a list of ways to achieve this item. Like the Dream List, realistic and outrageous ways to achieve this item are all welcome. You want to have an enormous list. Quantity of ideas is your objective.

Ways to Achieve My Dream List Item . . .

_____

_____

_____

_____

_____

_____

Review your list of ways to achieve your Dream List item. Circle the ideas that are most realistic and effective to achieve your Dream List item.

Your Dream List item will become a goal when it is written in specific, measureable and achievable terms. For example, you may want to have more financial security. The words "be rich" are not a goal. This is not specific, measurable or achievable. You need to determine how much is rich. Is it $500? $5,000? $50,000? $500,000? Or more? Determining an amount and writing that amount makes the Dream List more specific, measurable and achievable.

You may want to review those items you identified as your values and the current situation in your life to help determine the specifics to write your goal.

Please write the Dream List item in specific, measurable and achievable terms.

_____

_____

_____

_____

You also need to assign a realistic target time for completing the item. This makes the item measurable and achievable. Please include a specific target time in your goal. For example, the financial security item be rich may become the following specific, measurable and achievable goal…

To deposit a total of $5,000 in my savings account by August next year.

You now have a specific, measurable and achievable goal.

3. Consider the effects

The goal will impact or affect you and others. This step helps you maximize your resources and create a well-planned path to achieve your goal.

Are you the only person who needs to know about the goal?   Yes   No

Who else could help you achieve this goal?

_____

Who will be affected by this goal?

_____

To Whom should you share this goal?

_____

4. Reward yourself

The goal setting process is a day-to-day program. Every day you should review your goals. It's important to reward each small step you make toward achieving your goal. But first you need to identify these small steps.

Let's use the example of the financial goal. To deposit a total of $5,000 in my savings account by August next year. This goal can be considered in many small steps. For example, reaching the first $500 could be your first marker of small success toward the goal.

List the events (or changes) you consider indications of progress toward achieving your goal that you will reward.

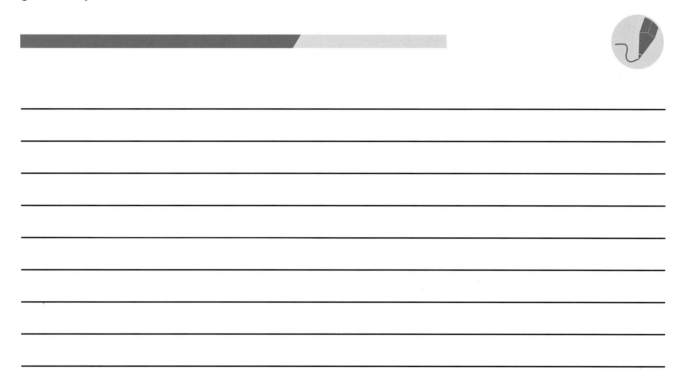

_____

_____

_____

_____

_____

_____

_____

_____

**The key to working smarter
is knowing the difference
between motion and direction.**

Motivation

There is so much hype about motivation. Some people claim to be great motivators. Sportscasters often talk about coaches motivating team members. But individual team members, just like you, decide what they do. Individuals motivate themselves. You may be inspired by others, but you make your own decisions to act. Whatever you choose to do is your decision.

Consider this…

Someone you do not know asks you to do something horrible. Do you do it? Probably not.

Someone you do not know points a gun to your head and tells you to do the same horrible thing. Do you do it? If it means your life, probably.

In both situations, the same request was made. In one situation, you refused the request; in one you agreed. They key point is YOU made the final decision.

Motivation is in all of us, but we are all motivated by different things. We have to work/play hard enough to find the best ways to motivate ourselves to reach the positive results we want. It's a personal choice and a personal adventure.

Here are a few places to start your adventure…

Liven-up with positive music you select

At some time, you've heard a crazy commercial jingle that stuck in your mind. Somehow, even hours after hearing the tune, you were still humming that little jingle. Your mind absorbs what it hears. It doesn't forget the inputs you provide. You fed your mind that crazy jingle. Choose the music you want that gives you positive messages and inspiration.

A speaking colleague, Kelly Barnes often asks audience members to find their personal song. Think about what song you'd pick as your theme song. Maybe when you're challenged with some negative happenings you should sing your own theme song as your positive background music.

Choose to spend time with positive people

You know people who are usually positive and people who are usually negative. You choose which people – positive or negative – you share your time. You are subjected to many external forces. Unfortunately, sometimes you must spend time with some people who are negative. But do you know you have a choice in selecting most of your surroundings? This includes the friends you regularly associate. Be choosey of how you spend your time. You're worth it!

Feed your mind with positive reading material

Your mind absorbs whatever you read. As you read, you are literally programming your mind. Reading at least a small sample of positive, inspirational material can be very energizing. Google stories about your favorite hobbies to find inspirational material to energize yourself.

Invest your free time

We *spend* a lot of our time, instead of always choosing to *invest* our time. We need to make a conscious effort to invest our free time in things that reward us. Are you just watching some TV or are you really watching something that is giving you satisfaction?

These are four simple starting points. Only you know what excites, what motivates, what inspires you.

What kind of energy/information are you absorbing from the world – positive or negative?

> **"Desire is the vehicle.**
> **Motivation is the engine.**
> **Discipline is the fuel."**
> **– C. Leslie Charles**

WIN

What's Important Now?

So much of our time and energy is focused on winning. Our examples of overcoming challenges and succeeding are often explained in athletic terms. Well, here's an alternative approach to consider that will consistently put you in a better place to in fact WIN.

Whatever is happening in your personal life, professional life or on your team – consider WIN. WIN is an acronym for **W**hat's **I**mportant **N**ow? No matter how busy you are; how challenged you feel; or out of control the situation appears; taking a few moments to reflect is often the best use of your energy. Stop and consider

What's Important Now?

Personally, it is time to answer the question – What's Important Now?

_____

_____

_____

Professionally, it is time to answer the question – What's Important Now?

_____

_____

_____

Your leadership team also needs to answer the question – What's Important Now?

_____

_____

_____

Your answers will give you some real options to redirect your efforts. Good luck as you discover – **What's Important Now?**

Your Personal Leadership Qualities

Do you have the potential to become a dynamic leader? Yes, of course you do! But where are you now? This questionnaire will help you personally evaluate your leadership qualities and performance.

If you can definitely answer "yes" to any of the following items, mark an "X" next to the item. If you have some doubts, make a note below the item describing how you could improve your present and future leadership performance. To help identify the power of leadership and principles listed below, try to identify someone you know or have met who is an example of the principle.

Best wishes evaluating your personal leadership qualities!

Are you:

_____ Currently acting as an informal leader?

You may or may not have a formal leadership role, but how are you performing with or without a title? Are others relying upon you as a team accomplisher? Do people look to you for leadership?

_____

_____

_____

Who have you seen act as an informal leader?

_____

_____ A problem solver?

Have you demonstrated the ability to answer challenges and produce positive results? Have others asked you for advice when a challenge arises?

_____

_____

_____

Who have you seen act as a problem solver?

_____

_____ A positive role model?

Do you demonstrate personal integrity? Are you behaving as a good member and person, both inside and outside the organization? Do you actively give credit to others for their accomplishments?

_____

_____

_____

Who have you seen act as a positive role model?

_____

_____ Striving to become a better person/member?

Do you ask for comments about your leadership performance from others? Do you read and search for new information to make you a more effective leader?

_____

_____

_____

Who have you seen striving to become better?

_____

_____ A volunteer?

Do you regularly volunteer to help others in and/or outside your group? Do others recognize your willingness to help?

_____

_____

_____

Who have you seen act as a volunteer?

_____

_____ A diligent worker?

Do you diligently pursue your responsibilities? Do others know you are committed to your tasks?

_____

_____

_____

Who have you seen act as a diligent worker?

_____

_____ A team player?

Can you graciously accept delegated responsibilities? Do you recognize and show your commitment to the organization? Do you involve others to help the organization grow?

_____

_____

_____

Who have you seen act as a team player?

_____

_____ Considerate of others?

Can you listen as well as you speak? Do you invite others to discuss their personal concerns with you? Do others consider you friendly?

_____

_____

_____

Who have you seen act considerate of others?

_____

"In order to plan your future wisely,
it is necessary that you understand
and appreciate your past."
– Jo Coudert

"People grow through experience
if they meet life honestly and courageously.
This is how character is built."
– Eleanor Roosevelt.

!

Discovering the Personal Power of Leadership

Leaders That Matter – Personal Coaches and Mentors

A Leader?

leader (lead'er), n.
1. a person or thing that leads; directing, commanding, or guiding head, as of a group or activity.

A Person That Leads?

lead (led), v.
1. to guide by holding the hand, pulling a rope, etc.
2. to guide or conduct by showing the way; to guide the course or direction of.
3. to conduct, as a chief or commander; to direct and govern.
4. to precede; to introduce by going first.
5. to hold the first place in rank or dignity among.
6. to show the method of attaining an object; to direct, as in an investigation.

Yes, all these define the act of leading. And you can probably think of an example for all six definitions. These examples are what make a difference for you. These personal examples move you beyond the definitions. These are the moments of leadership when your life is touched by another person.

There is so much talk and writing about leaders. Who are these leaders? What is a leader? Do you become a leader just by being elected to office? Are leaders good followers? Are leaders only positive? Can leaders be negative? Who decides who or what is a leader? Hmmm!

Everyone has been influenced by someone. Beyond the buzzwords and case studies, leadership is personal. The most powerful leadership examples are those that touch your life.

Try this short exercise to discover the personal power of leaders and leadership.

1. Remember your leaders.
2. Identify their specific leadership characteristics.
3. Recall how they used these characteristics.
4. Identify your specific leadership characteristics.
5. Recall how you have used these characteristics.
6. Commit to share and develop your gift of leadership.

First, remember individuals who were/are leaders, mentors, teachers or coaches. Don't worry about picking THE leader. The more names you write, the more examples you have to choose. Simply write down anyone who has affected you in some way. The leaders can be individuals or groups you know very well or only know their reputation. These individuals, groups or institutions, whether they are deceased or living, fictional or non-fictional, have affected you in some way.

Are you challenged remembering anyone or any group? Try this…close your eyes and remember your favorite teacher's smile and how good they made you feel…that should jump-start your memory.

My Leaders – Personal Mentors & Coaches

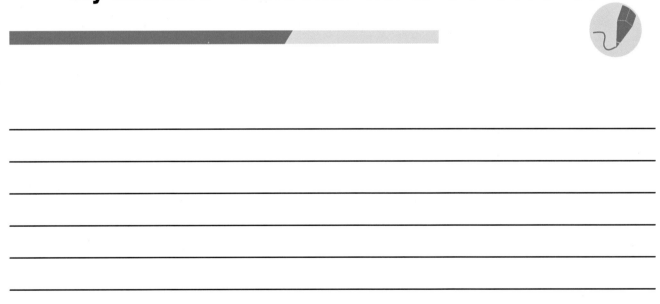

Select the two or three leaders, mentors or coaches from the list you create who had the biggest impact on you. Write the names of these special people under Leaders/Mentors/Coaches.

Second, identify their specific or outstanding leadership characteristics. What is it that made them so special? Were they a wonderful encourager? Did they tell great stories? Did they make other people feel important? Were they extremely patient? List these special characteristics.

Leaders/Mentors/Coaches	Special Characteristics	Special Moments

Third, recall specific moments, events or instances when your leaders used or shared each of these characteristics. The event may be a historical moment for the world or a personal moment you shared with one of your leaders. List these specific moments on the right-hand side beside the characteristics.

Often people touch our lives with what they do or say. We feel good from the positive experience. Looking at why people make us feel special or why we're inspired by others helps us become better leaders. Your mentor or coach may be someone very famous or someone known by few people. Fame doesn't make a leader. Leadership is personal.

The next step is to take a closer look at yourself. How have you served as a leader of yourself and a coach or mentor for others? You have several skills that you should appreciate.

> "We all live in suspense, from day to day, from hour to hour; in other words, we are the hero of our own story."
> – Mary McCarthy

Fourth, identify your specific leadership characteristics. What are some of your personal leadership characteristics? List your leadership characteristics on the left. Are you a good listener? Are you slow to judge others? Do you have a great sense of humor? Are you diligent? Do you smile often? Do people know you care? List as many qualities or characteristics as you want.

My Leadership Characteristics   *Special Moments*

_____

_____

_____

_____

_____

_____

Fifth, recall how you used each of your special characteristics. List these moments beside each of the characteristics under Special Moments. Consider all people and parts of your life…family, friends, school and work. Leadership is personal and it happens everywhere.

For example, one of your many leadership characteristics may be your great listening skills. Recall a moment when you used your listening skills. Maybe you were in a heated debate with someone. Instead of trying to change the other person's mind, you stopped arguing and really listened. You used your listening skills to resolve conflict. This could be one of the specific moments you used one of your leadership characteristics.

Sixth, commit to share and develop your leadership gift. Now that you've invested the time and thought about leadership characteristics, what can you do today and every day to make a difference? What special characteristics do you have to share with the world?

> # Leadership is…
> ## Courage to adjust mistakes, vision to welcome chance, and confidence to stay out of step when everyone else is marching to the wrong tune.

Mentor Moments Log

Deciding to develop your leadership skills is a big commitment. One wonderful tool to keep you focused on the commitment is to create a *Mentor Moments Log*. A *Mentor Moments Log* is simply a diary of good stuff – the moments when people choose to make a difference.

Leadership is all around us. Look for it and appreciate it when you see it. Leadership includes the magnificent to the miniscule. If we keep looking for the good, we're focused on the positive. When you start to see the impact of these mentor moments you'll see the power of leadership. The greatest benefit is when you begin to feel or internalize this power and start to exercise your power to make a difference in every moment.

The *Mentor Moments Log* can be part of this <u>A Leadership Experience</u> guide. Add some paper to the back of the book. Capture those moments when you see yourself and other leaders impacting others. Celebrate when you see people do good things for others.

Inspirational Quote Collection

These famous and not-so-famous quotes about leadership are offered as inspiration to help you feel the power of your leadership abilities. They're a reminder that leadership is personal. Use these as the beginning of your inspirational quote collection.

"When you cease to make a contribution, you begin to die."
– Eleanor Roosevelt

Good leaders take a little more than their share of the blame, a little less than their share of the credit.

"You are not here merely to make a living. You are here in order to enable the world to live more amply, with greater vision, with a finer spirit of hope and achievement. You are here to enrich the world, and you impoverish yourself if you forget the errand."
– Woodrow Wilson

Leaders are ordinary people with extraordinary determination.

Leaders are those who have two characteristics: first, they are going somewhere; second, they are able to persuade other people to go with them.

"What one does is what counts and not what one had the intention of doing."
– Pablo Picasso

"A title, however, makes no one a leader."
– Hap Klopp

*"You cannot be a leader, and ask other people to follow you,
unless you know how to follow, too."*
– Sam Rayburn

*Good leaders inspire others to have confidence in them;
Great leaders inspire others to have confidence in themselves.*

"Be the change you want to see in the world."
– Gandhi

*"The last of the human freedoms – to choose one's attitude in any
given set of circumstances, to choose one's own way."*
– Viktor Frankl

"Here's a simple approach to creativity: Look at more stuff; think about it harder."
– Geof Hammond

"Think wrongly if you please, but in all cases think for yourself."
– Louisa May Alcott

"I think the one lesson I have learned is that there is no substitution for paying attention."
– Diane Sawyer

What Have You Been Dealt?

This *What Have You Been Dealt?* exercise is designed to help individuals learn about their beliefs and values. Traditional education usually doesn't ask us to examine why we hold certain beliefs. This module helps individuals reflect on not only what they believe but also the origin of those beliefs.

> **"There is something in every one of you that waits and listens for the sound of the genuine in yourself."**
> **– Howard Truman**

What Have You Been Dealt? can also help strengthen teams. Working with others is often challenging. The greater the task, the greater the need for strong, trusting relationships. It is also important to understand ourselves. Investing time to learn about others when we start working together is a way to increase our chance of success.

What Have You Been Dealt? can be used in a variety of ways. It is first and foremost a self-discovery tool, but it can also help forge strong team relationships. The more we learn about one another, the greater the opportunity to accomplish more difficult challenges.

The eight areas of focus are –

Major Events	Physical Environment
Politics	Friends/Peers/Confidants
Family	School/Teachers/Students
Spiritual	Other Influences

Here are ways to use What Have You Been Dealt? The eight main topics are listed below and you can write on the lines provided. But it is very fun to write each topic on a note "card" with your answers. These become the "cards" you are dealt.

Individually

The cards are always individually completed. Individuals are asked to write short phrases describing the significant contributors to their beliefs, whether they are people or institutions or experiences. It is helpful to think of different stages of your life while completing the cards. The cards can be completed in a short period of 15-30 minutes. Or it can be a more thorough process where individuals continue to list contributions on their cards for several weeks. The process of independently completing the exercise may be enough without sharing.

Some Disclosure

After everyone has information on their What Have You Been Dealt? cards, individuals are asked to look through their cards and circle what they believe are the strongest impressions or contributions to their lives. This is followed by each person simply sharing what they circled.

> "It is rewarding to find someone you like, but it is essential to like yourself . . . It is a delight to discover people who are worthy of respect and admiration and love, but it is vital to believe yourself deserving of these things."
> – Jo Coudert

Lengthy Discussion & Questions

After everyone has completed the exercise an intense discussion follows. It is helpful to stay focused by having one person designated as the facilitator or give everyone the right to interject a phrase such as "Back to the Purpose" or "Tangent" or "Squirrel." Sample questions to ask:

- Which cards have the most significant items listed?
- What card was the most difficult to complete? Why?
- Which item listed are you most proud? Why?
- Which item listed has caused you the most frustration? Why?
- Which card would you like to have more information listed? Why?
- What was an important realization you had during this exercise?

These are only a few questions to share. The most important part of the process is self-discovery. This is a safe process for individuals to look at what and why they believe.

> "I am part of all that I have met;
> yet all experience is an arch where
> through gleams that untraveled world
> whose margin fades for ever and for
> ever when I move."
> – Alfred, Lord Tennyson

Major Events

(National/World Events, Media Influence)

_____

_____

_____

_____

_____

Physical Environment

(Home, Community, School)

_____

_____

_____

_____

_____

Politics

(Family party beliefs; Hometown political figure)

_____

_____

_____

_____

_____

_____

Other Influences

_____

_____

_____

_____

_____

_____

Friends/Peers/Confidants

_____

_____

_____

_____

_____

Schools/Teachers/Students

_____

_____

_____

_____

_____

_____

Family

_____

_____

_____

_____

_____

_____

Spiritual

_____

_____

_____

_____

_____

_____

What do You Value?
Finding Balance in Your Life

Values? Hmmmmmm?!

value (val'u)
1. that quality of a thing according to which it is thought of as being more or less desirable, useful, estimable, or important; worth or the degree of worth.

It's NOT prestige. It's NOT money. It's NOT popularity.

Values are more important than prestige, money or popularity. Values are personal. They are what and where you place your life emphasis. Yes, values are a bit abstract and intangible. Values are hard to describe, but they shine through in every word and deed.

Sometimes you may feel or sense being out of synch or in a rut. These feelings may be your body telling you that you're not living what you value. You're living a life in accordance with your values when you feel balanced and satisfied.

Our culture rewards individuals who are on the fast track – getting more done in less time. Here is the bigger question: Is the fast track the right track for you? Only you can answer that question.

It's such a temptation to push and push and push. With each new techno gadget and upgrade it's nearly addicting to push harder. At what point does the process take control over us? Tap the brakes and invest the time to explore your own values and momentum before you spin out of control. Discovering and living your values are ways you can create a positive balance in your life.

Why should you find your balance?

1. It keeps you healthy and happy.
2. A healthier you is a better servant to those you share leadership responsibilities.

Finding your natural momentum or pace and balance is a challenge. It requires time and honest examination to discover your balance. Focusing on positive experiences or periods helps you understand yourself. Identifying what was happening at those times helps you discover what you value. Here are four steps to guide you.

1. Identify Those Moments of Peace.

Operating outside of your natural or comfortable ranges for prolonged periods makes you feel out of balance or out of synch. You may even feel ill, somewhat depressed or irritable as a symptom of operating out of your natural zone or living without focusing on your values.

Ask yourself these questions to recall when you felt in control or at peace. It's important to write at least a few words to answer every question.

- When was the last time I felt joy?
- When did I feel at peace?
- What do I have fond memories of in the past five years?
- Who/what has made me smile the most?
- When was the last time I felt I had control over my life?

> ## "It is not by muscle, speed, or physical dexterity that great things are achieved, but by reflection, force of character and judgment."
> ## – Cicero

2. Identify Where You Were Operating on the Continuum.

MILD   **MEDIUM**   **HOT**

The names *mild, medium* and *hot* are used to explain the intensity of how you operate or the momentum you use to complete your responsibilities. We all operate at different points along the continuum for different reasons. For example: After recovering from an illness you may physically need to stay in the *mild* range. When faced with a pressing deadline, you may need to operate in the extreme *hot* range.

A word of caution about the continuum: regardless of where someone comfortably operates, no range is better than another and no range has less of a work ethic than another. It's simply the momentum with which we move.

132

For each of the moments or periods you identified above, circle where you were operating on the continuum.

The last time I felt joy?	MILD	MEDIUM	HOT
When I felt at peace?	MILD	MEDIUM	HOT
What I have fond memories of in the past five years?	MILD	MEDIUM	HOT
Who/what made me smile the most?	MILD	MEDIUM	HOT
The last time I felt I had control over my life?	MILD	MEDIUM	HOT

Your responses may show some patterns. Are the ranges of mild, medium and hot you circled skewed to one part of the continuum?

3. Identify What Else Was Happening.

In those moments of peace or those periods of control identify what else was happening in your life. Here are some statements to help you explore the other events that helped shape these moments or periods. Complete the statements for each of the moments or periods you identified above.

The last time I felt joy was: _____

I felt good about my friendships because: _____

_____

I felt good about my family relationships because: _____

_____

I felt good about myself because: _____

_____

I felt at peace when: _____

I felt good about my friendships because: _____

_____

I felt good about my family relationships because: _____

_____

I felt good about myself because: _____

_____

In the past five years I have fond memories of: _____

_____

I felt good about my friendships because: _____

_____

I felt good about my family relationships because: _____

_____

I felt good about myself because: _____

_____

The people or thing that made me smile the most is/was: _____

_____

I felt good about my friendships because: _____

_____

I felt good about my family relationships because: _____

_____

I felt good about myself because: _____

_____

The last time I felt I had control over my life was: _____

_____

I felt good about my friendships because: _____

_____

I felt good about my family relationships because: _____

_____

I felt good about myself because: _____

_____

The statements point to your feelings of comfort at different periods of your life. Considering where you were operating on the continuum and what was happening in your life connects the head and the heart. It helps make sense of how to best accomplish your responsibilities and maintain your mental and physical health. When you feel balanced, you are living in accordance with your values.

> ## "Nothing said to us, Nothing we can learn from others, Reaches us so deep As that which we find in ourselves."
> ## – Theodore Reik

4. Identify Adjustments to Make.

Too many hard-working people are burning out by pushing themselves out of their comfortable range. Stop feeling frazzled and make adjustments. Here are some questions to help you clarify your values and find your balance.

Do you feel you have control over your life? _____

In what areas/responsibilities do you practice your control or management?_____
_____

Is there some activity or responsibility you could eliminate?_____
_____

Why are you successful?_____
_____

What frustrates you must? _____
_____

What makes you the most proud?_____
_____

Your values are what you believe is most worthy in life. Investing the time to see what you value helps you understand yourself. You feel balance when you are living your life in accordance with your values and operating in your natural or comfortable range. That is success!

> "It's never too late in fiction
> or in life – to revise."
> – Nancy Thayer

Listening Skills for Leaders

Listen for what interests others

It's easy to learn what interests others. If you carefully listen and remember what people say, you'll communicate better. Listening and remembering what others say gives you important conversation starters.

Remember how uncomfortable you've felt when a group disbanded and you were left with nothing to say to another person. If you listen and remember the interests of others, you'll have perfect conversation starters.

Remember people's names and use them often

Nothing is more precious than hearing your own name. It feels good when people remember your name, and people appreciate you remembering their name. When you call someone by their name, they listen to you because you've paid value to them. This is a wonderful attention getter. No matter how brief your encounter with someone, remember their name in conversation and commit it to memory…you'll make people feel special.

Listen and capitalize on agreement

Good conversation builds relationships. Emphasizing points of agreement and similarities builds communication. Whenever you and the other person have agreed on something, restate the point. Amplifying points of agreement encourages more conversation.

Use pulse points to initiate conversation and gain attention

A pulse point is a sensitive or important focus of an individual's life – a particular sport, hobby or issue. As a keen observer, use pulse points to initiate conversation and gain attention.

For example: If you're introduced to a man wearing a suit and tie, you may simply have a boring conversation about the weather. But if you were searching for pulse points, you'd notice the man's lapel pin in the shape of a gold club. Immediately you have a prime topic for conversation – golf. Talking about golf would instantly gain the man's interest.

Pulse points are used by successful conversationalists to make people feel comfortable and important. People are happy to share their comments on topics they enjoy.

Talk about others, not yourself

Encourage others to talk about themselves. Comments such as "What do you think about…?" or "How do you feel about…?" are open-ended questions. These encourage people to talk about what they think or feel. Whenever a conversation seems to lag, use an open-ended question. You'll be amazed how much people enjoy talking about themselves and what they believe.

Listen to what you are saying

Be conscious of what you say, both verbally and nonverbally.

Listening to your own communication will make you a better communicator. As you listen to your own communication, you'll become more involved in conversations. Ask yourself these questions to check your performance as a communicator…

Is my body sending a positive message to others?
Am I using positive words and phrases in conversation?
Am I making the other person feel comfortable?

"The real spirit of conversation consists in building on another's observations, not overturning it."
– Edward G. Bulwer-Lytton

Listening Self-Assessment

YES   SOMETIMES   NO   1.   Do you totally concentrate on the speaker's message, forgetting all of your concerns?

YES   SOMETIMES   NO   2.   Do you listen to the speaker even if you don't really like the speaker?

YES   SOMETIMES   NO   3.   Do you attentively listen even if you don't like the subject?

YES   SOMETIMES   NO   4.   Do you wait for another person to finish speaking before you begin?

YES   SOMETIMES   NO   5.   Do you wait to form an opinion until you have heard all that the speaker is saying?

YES   SOMETIMES   NO   6.   Do you try to understand why the speaker is delivering the message?

YES   SOMETIMES   NO   7.   Do you stop the task you are currently doing to give the speaker your full attention?

YES   SOMETIMES   NO   8.   Do you believe you can improve your listening skills?

YES   SOMETIMES   NO   9.   Do you enjoy listening to others?

YES   SOMETIMES   NO   10.   Do you restate the speaker's message to make certain you properly understand the message?

YES   SOMETIMES   NO   11.   Do you encourage the speaker to continue speaking by sending positive feedback?

YES   SOMETIMES   NO   12.   Do you ask constructive questions to encourage the speaker to provide more information to fully convey the message?

YES   SOMETIMES   NO   13.   Do you listen to the speaker's message instead of the speaker's style and vocabulary?

YES   SOMETIMES   NO   14.   Do people often talk to you about what is on their mind?

YES   SOMETIMES   NO   15.   Does your relationship with the speaker affect how well you listen? (i.e. Do you listen more intently to a friend than a stranger?)

YES   SOMETIMES   NO   16.   Does the age of the speaker affect how well you listen?

YES   SOMETIMES   NO   17.   Do you offer feedback to the speaker, nodding, smiling and showing enthusiasm?

YES   SOMETIMES   NO   18. Do you continue to listen even though you think you know what is going to be said?

YES   SOMETIMES   NO   19. Do you try to read between the lines to really understand what the speaker is saying?

YES   SOMETIMES   NO   20. Do you ask for clarification of unfamiliar words and terms?

YES   SOMETIMES   NO   21. Do you ignore distractions around you?

There are no right or wrong answers to this assessment. This is only an evaluation of what you perceive as your current listening strengths and potential shortcomings. As a leader, it is very important to evaluate how you are communicating with others. If there were some items you answered "no" or "sometimes", or items you carefully considered before answering "yes," congratulations! You've identified some important areas for potential improvement.

This assessment is the first step. How, where and when you choose to make changes is your decision.

> **"There is nothing with which every person is so afraid as getting to know how enormously much they are capable of doing and becoming."**
> **– Soren Kierkegaard**

Leadership Strengths Inventory

It's a good practice to explore your strengths to understand your natural tendencies. These strengths are the gifts you have to share with the world. There are many tools to help you identify your strengths and tendencies – Gallup Clifton StrengthsFinder, Myers-Briggs, DiSC, True Colors, Strengths Deployment Triangle, and more.

A wonderful tool for young student leaders is CliftonStrengths for Students. The book includes a unique access code to take the CliftonStrengths Assessment and specific directions for where your strengths might be a good fit as you pursue your education.

This Leadership Strengths Inventory below helps you see what is obvious for you. There is not an answer key. This is a reflection tool to help you bring your strengths to the surface. It may sound silly but you are with yourself all the time. So much of what you do becomes routine or habit. When you get into your routine of simply going through the motions, you often set yourselves on auto-pilot.

Your challenge is to first read all of the 22 words below. Then circle the four words which are your strongest leadership qualities. After you circle only four words, then rank those four items from 1 to 4 (1 being your strongest quality, 2 being your second strongest quality and so on.) Remember – you can only select four, so choose carefully.

____ Approachable	____ Change-Agent	____ Conceptual
____ Conversationalist	____ Detailed	____ Enthusiastic
____ Flexible	____ Focused	____ Humorous
____ Initiator	____ Inspirational	____ Learner
____ Level-Headed	____ Organized	____ Persistent
____ Positive	____ Public Speaker	____ Responsible
____ Role Model	____ Strategist	____ Supportive
____ Worker		

Leadership Characteristics to Master

"Wow, President John F. Kennedy was a charismatic leader! People were spellbound by his speeches. He was a real leader with a magnetic personality. I wish I had been born a leader. I wish I had a personality that attracted others."

Surprise! Leadership is sometimes mistakenly considered an inborn talent. President Kennedy was not born a leader; he carefully shaped his leadership skills. Leadership can be developed by anyone with a sincere desire to become a successful, dynamic leader.

"How can I develop my leadership skills?"

Successful people have found a special blend of leadership characteristics, they live inside-out. They value people and good deeds. Dynamic leaders value some common characteristics. Studying and practicing these common characteristics will help you recognize your own skills and build your leadership abilities.

Show enthusiasm every day

Enthusiasm is contagious energy. People enjoy working or sharing with enthusiastic people.

Surround yourself with positive people

Show discretion when selecting friends. Don't subject yourself to negative influences. Some people haven't learned the joy of being optimistic. These people expect the negative and make a point to bring others down to a pessimistic attitude. Time you invest with others should be a growing and learning experience. Be selective.

Don't boast or brag

Successful leaders amplify the good deeds of others, not their own. People admire and respect the charismatic leader. When charismatic leaders are paid a compliment, they simply say "thank you." These leaders do not need to talk about the deed or situation. The good result or achievement is the greatest satisfaction these leaders can receive. Remember – *Good leaders take a little more than their share of the blame, a little less than their share of the credit.*

Don't be a trend follower

Decide what you want to pursue. Satisfaction cannot come from the exterior world. Everyone must find what makes them happy. Individuals, who constantly follow the latest trends and fads, changing their lifestyles to fit the behavior of others, are not leaders. They are followers.

Use a positive, motivating vocabulary

Leaders may speak often or very seldom, but they speak in a positive, motivating language. Many people are very critical of their own behavior. Successful leaders recognize that people don't need more cynicism, they need support and encouragement. A positive, motivating vocabulary builds respect and strength. Examples of a vocabulary turned to the positive, motivating

Negative	Positive
• I, me, my	• You, us, we
• If only	• Next time
• Problem	• Challenge
• Failure	• Temporary setback
• Soon	• Today
• Difficult	• Interesting

Expect the best

Individuals who others may view as "lucky" are often simply successful. The "lucky" people always seem to have things go well for them. Contrary to common belief, these people are only reaping the benefits of the opportunities they have created for themselves. Successful people make success a habit. They expect the best to happen because they always contribute their best. Make success your habit!

Leadership is the result of attitudes, as well as characteristics. It requires practice to develop positive leadership skills and courage to shine as the best you can possibly be at all times.

> "The greatest gift
> we can bestow on others
> is a good example."
> – Thomas Morell

Ethics

The study of standards of conduct and moral judgment.
The study of morals of a particular person, religion, group, etc.

Ethics are the landmark of high character. Respectable leaders always try to demonstrate ethical behavior. As leaders we must expect the best behavior from ourselves and others. The following questions are an excellent review of our expectations of ethical behavior. Share the questions and your responses with other group members. It's fun and you may be surprised at what you discover.

What would you do if...

You bought a new, expensive jacket, but the sales clerk charged you less than the ticket price? You realize this when you get home.

Your extremely wealthy aunt, who you don't particularly like, becomes ill and wants to leave you her money? What do you do?

At an important banquet honoring professionals a group member arrives wearing blue jeans which is not allowed in your official dress code? What do you do?

You are required to attend the state conference as a chapter president, but the basketball game for the conference championship is the same night and you are the team's star player? What do you do?

You don't like any of the political candidates or their platforms. Would you vote?

You find some creative ideas for a presentation, but the materials are copyrighted. Would you use the materials anyway?

A classmate has missed class for three weeks with no excuse for the absence. Do you let him/her copy your notes?

You suspect your neighbors are abusing their children. Do you report them to the authorities?

You witness a car accident and know one person is at fault.
Do you tell the authorities?

You arrive at an isolated intersection at 2:30 AM. Do you drive through the red light?

You see your neighbor, who has been unemployed for three months, shoplifting groceries? What do you do?

You accidentally dent another car in a parking lot and no one sees you? What do you do?

An employee asks you to write a reference for him/her. He/she has been a bad worker. Do you write the reference?

You drive by a man waving frantically on the side of the road late at night. Do you stop?

A group member was responsible for mailing invitations to guests for an important banquet. As the committee chair, you learn that two prominent officials didn't receive invitations. What do you do?

No one sees you accidentally back into a large display which comes crashing to the floor at the grocery store. Do you leave?

You didn't use a cart at the grocery store and innocently placed a few items in your pocket when your arms were full. You discover the items when you return home. What do you do?

A friendly waitress does her best to satisfy you, but the food doesn't arrive at your table for an hour. Do you tip the waitress?

Your friend gives you quarters to play a slot machine. You win $250. What do you do with the winnings?

A co-worker has terribly bad breath. Do you tell him/her?

You are unemployed and have nowhere to go for help. Do you steal food?

You see your mom cheating (claiming more expenses that she is entitled) on her expense account. Do you say anything to her?

An exclusive community organization has offered you a two-year membership. You're enthusiastic about the organization. Two months later you learn that the organization discriminates. Do you continue your membership?

An ATM gives you an additional $40 which cannot be traced. Do you keep the money?

You and your friends have planned for three years to live together after graduation. Two other friends offer you a golden opportunity to live with them in a beautiful apartment at a very reasonable price. What do you do?

You are paid a fee for a presentation you deliver. There is no way to trace the income. Do you declare the fee on your income tax return?

You work for a chemical company that is illegally treating chemicals to save money. Do you report the illegal activity and risk losing your job?

The answers to these questions are not always easy. There are many gray areas. Ethical dilemmas may arise whenever there is potential profit or personal gain that will negatively affect others. It may be tempting to recap the short term benefits, but the results will become a permanent mark on the individual's reputation.

How ethical were your responses to these questions? As a leader, what reputation would you have if you had in fact actually carried out your responses?

Reporters, newscasters and headlines inform us of the unethical behavior in professional and personal life. Some of these unethical events have been insider stock trading scandals, adultery, toxic waste dumping and political bribery. These reports have raised the public's concern. In fact, people are very skeptical of government, business, and leaders of organizations.

As creatures of habit we recognize the truth of the statement – "Monkey see, monkey do." Successful leaders are examples of positive, ethical behavior. Leaders have a responsibility to those they lead, the environment, the community, the nation and the world. Successful leaders have set a high standard for themselves and others.

Leadership is responsibility; a responsibility to make decisions and act in the best interests of others. Ethical behavior is the courageous, responsible choice!

It's extremely difficult to lead farther than you have gone yourself.

Attitude Assessment

YES	**NO**	1. Do you consistently demonstrate your trust in others and their abilities?
YES	**NO**	2. Do you give others small gifts or cards to show them your appreciation?
YES	**NO**	3. Do others know you will go the extra mile to help them?
YES	**NO**	4. Do you always have a cheerful expression?
YES	**NO**	5. Do you help others realize their potential?
YES	**NO**	6. Do you generate enthusiasm in others?
YES	**NO**	7. Do you always strive for excellence?
YES	**NO**	8. Do you help others understand themselves?
YES	**NO**	9. Do you discipline yourself to form positive habits?
YES	**NO**	10. Do you practice a consistent recognition system to acknowledge the accomplishment of others?
YES	**NO**	11. Do you consciously use positive words, phrases, and expressions when working with others?
YES	**NO**	12. Do you share your time and thoughts with others because you sincerely care about them?
YES	**NO**	13. Do you attentively listen to others?
YES	**NO**	14. Do you understand how much influence you have on others?
YES	**NO**	15. Do you demonstrate dependability in all of your responsibilities?
YES	**NO**	16. Do you find sincere compliments to give others?
YES	**NO**	17. Do you practice a synergistic attitude in your team responsibilities?
YES	**NO**	18. Do you help others implement positive, healthy attitudes of themselves and their work?
YES	**NO**	19. Do you truly respect your great country and the free enterprise system?
YES	**NO**	20. Do you strive to create an environment that builds others?

There are no right or wrong answers to this assessment. This is only an evaluation of what you perceive as your current strengths and potential shortcomings. As a leader it is very important to evaluate how you are interacting with others. If there were some items you answered "no" or items you carefully considered before answering "yes," congratulations! You've identified areas for potential improvement.

This evaluation is the first step. How, where and when you choose to make changes is your decision.

> "Always bear in mind that your own resolution to success is more important than any other one thing."
> – Abraham Lincoln

INSPIRATION

Patty Hendrickson™

INSPIRING LEADERS

Your Quote Collection

You may be asked to speak when you least expect the invitation. Prepare for these unexpected invitations to deliver a quality presentation. You may only speak for 30 seconds, but you want to say something worthwhile. You may not have access to resources when you're asked, so plan ahead for the unexpected. The following are a few of our favorites to help you start your quote and story collection. Reading the quotes are also an excellent way to brighten your day if you're feeling particularly challenged.

*"To be what we are, and to become what we are capable of becoming,
is the only end of life."*
– Robert Louis Stevenson

*"Success…seems to be connected with action. Successful people keep
moving. They make mistakes, but they don't quit."*
– Conrad Hilton

*"The highest reward for a person's toil is not what they get for it,
but what they become by it."*
– John Ruskin

*"The only thing we have to bring to community is ourselves, so the
contemplative process of recovering our true selves in solitude is never selfish.
It is ultimately the best gift we can give others."*
– Parker Palmer

*"Far away there in the sunshine are my highest aspirations.
I may not reach them, but I can look up and see their beauty,
believe in them and try to follow where they lead."*
– Louisa May Alcott

"One can never consent to creep when one feels an impulse to soar."
– Helen Keller

*"Driving around in circles may make your speedometer look impressive,
but it won't get you across the country very fast."*
– Seth Godin

*"Here's a simple approach to creativity:
Look at more stuff; think about it harder."*
– Geof Hammond

"One of the easiest ways to change is simply to alter your position – to focus on the one-inch square in front of you and put one foot in front of the other. But to go forward – on a cliff, on a project, or in your career – you sometimes first have to take steps sideways, or even a step back."
– Mike Donahue

"We do not see ideas with our eyes. We see them with our minds."
– Robert Kiyosaki

"Thoughts are energy. And you can make your world or break your world by thinking."
– Susan L. Taylor

"If you're trying to do something really well, you're constantly questioning yourself. Self-doubt, I think is what it is. To renew and reaffirm what you do, you have to do it on a daily basis."
– Yo Yo Ma

"Don't focus on building up your weaknesses. Understand your strengths and place yourself in a position where these strengths count. Your strengths are what will carry you through to success."
– Peter Drucker

"To focus on personality before character is to try to grow the leaves without the roots."
– Stephen Covey

"Learning is meant to be – active, passionate, and personal."
– Warren Bennis

"In creative action, our desire is not to 'solve' or 'succeed' or 'survive,' but to give birth to something new."
– Parker Palmer

"The person who sees the world at 50 the same way they saw it at 20 has wasted 30 years of their life."
– Muhammad Ali

"It is only when we harness the power of our collective consciousness that we can rid ourselves of the horrible things in this world that we presently accept as just the way things are."
– Marianne Williamson

*"A happy person is not a person in a certain set of circumstances,
but rather a person with a certain set of attitudes."*
– Hugh Downs

"If you want to live a happy life, tie it to a goal, not to people or things."
– Albert Einstein

"Those who smile rather than rage are always stronger."
– Japanese Proverb

*"Nothing great is created suddenly, any more than a bunch of grapes or a fig. If
you tell me that you desire a fig, I answer you that there must be time.
Let it first blossom, then bear fruit, then ripen."*
– Epictetus

*"If you're not speaking your own truth, you will never be able to be all you are
meant to be. You cannot be pretending to be somebody else."*
– Oprah Winfrey

*"Whatever the world may say or do, my part is to keep myself good; just as a
gold piece, or an emerald, or a purple robe insists perpetually, 'Whatever the
world may say or do, my part is to remain an emerald and keep my color true.' "*
– Marcus Aurelius

*"The greater danger for most of us isn't that our aim is too high and miss it,
but that it is too low and we reach it."*
– Michelangelo

*"To laugh often and much; to win the respect of intelligent people and the
affection of children; to earn the appreciation of honest critics and endure the
betrayal of false friends; to appreciate beauty; to find the best in others; to leave
the world a bit better, whether by a healthy child, a garden patch or a redeemed
social condition; to know even one life has breathed easier because you have
lived. This is to have succeeded."*
– Ralph Waldo Emerson

*"Happiness is when what you think, what you say,
and what you do are in harmony."*
– Mahatma Gandhi

*"If your lips would keep from slips,
Five things observe with care.
Of whom you speak, to whom you speak,
And how and when and where."*
– Unknown

*"Quality is never an accident; it is always the result of high intention,
sincere effort, intelligent direction and skillful execution;
it represents the wise choice of many alternatives."*
– Willa A. Foster

*"They may forget what you said,
but they will never forget how you made them feel."*
– Carl W. Buechner

*"We pay a heavy price for our fear of failure. It is a powerful
obstacle to growth. It assures the progressive narrowing of the
personality and prevents exploration and experimentation. There is no learning
without some difficulty and fumbling. If you want to keep on learning,
you must keep on risking failure – all of your life."*
– John W. Gardner

*"Only in growth, reform and change, paradoxically enough,
is true security to be found."*
– Anne Morrow Lindbergh

I"f you've only one breath left, use it to say 'thank you.' "
– Pam Brown

"When you have to make a choice and don't make it, that is in itself a choice."
– William James

*"The first responsibility of a leader is to define reality. The last is to say thank
you. In between the two, the leader must become a servant and debtor.
That sums up the progress of an artful leader."*
– Max DePree

*"Courage doesn't always roar. Sometimes courage is the little voice at the end
of the day that says 'I'll try again tomorrow.' "*
– Mary Anne Radmacher

*"The credit belongs to the person who is actually in the arena, who's face is
marred by dust and sweat and blood; who strives valiantly; who errs and comes
short again and again, who knows the great enthusiasm, the great devotions,
and spends their self in a worthy cause; who at the best, knows the triumph of
high achievement; and who, at the worst, if they fail, at least fail while daring
greatly, so that their place shall never be with those cold and timid souls who
know neither victory nor defeat."*
– Theodore Roosevelt

"What really matters is what you do with what you have."
– Shirley Lord

"The people who get on in this world are the people who get up and look for the circumstances they want, and, if they can't find them, make them."
– George Bernard Shaw

"What lies behind us and what lies before us are tiny matters compared to what lies within us."
– Ralph Waldo Emerson

"Progress always involves risk; you can't steal second base and keep your foot on first."
– Frederick Wilcox

"People with goals succeed because they know where they're going."
– Earl Nightingale

"An education isn't how much you have committed to memory, or even how much you know. It's being able to differentiate between what you do know and what you don't. It's knowing where to go to find out what you need to know; and it's knowing how to use the information you get."
– William Feather

"Success isn't a result of spontaneous combustion. You must set yourself on fire."
– Arnold Glasgow

"Joy is not in things; it is in us."
– Richard Wagner

"I have never given very deep thought to a philosophy of life though I have a few ideas that I think are useful to me: Do whatever comes your way as well as you can. Think as little as possible about yourself. Think as much as possible about other people."
– Eleanor Roosevelt

"With every deed you are sowing a seed, though the harvest you may not see."
– Ella Wheeler Wilcox

"Our lives begin to end the day we become silent about things that matter."
– Martin Luther King, Jr.

"An education isn't how much you have committed to memory, or even how much you know. It's being able to differentiate between what you do know and what you don't. It's knowing where to go to find out what you need to know; and it's knowing how to use the information you get."
– William Feather

"Without difficulties, life would be like a stream without rocks and curves – about as interesting as concrete. Without problems, there can be no personal growth, no group achievement, no progress for humanity."
– Benjamin Hoff

"Some times the smallest step in the right direction ends up being the biggest step of your life. Tiptoe is you must, but take the step."
– Naeem Callaway

"Whatever the job you are asked to do at whatever level, do your best, Because your reputation is your resume."
– Madeline Albright

"You can't be awesome and negative. So pick one!"
– David Mouser

These are beautiful quotes and a great starting point. Now it's your turn to start capturing those quotations that touch your heart. It's important to have a reliable place to turn for inspiration. Your personal quote collection can be that place. Enjoy!

Are YOU an Active Member?

Are you an active member,
the kind that would be missed?
Or are you just contented
that your name is on the list?

Do you attend the meeting,
and mingle with the flock?
Or do you stay at home
and criticize and knock?

Do you take an active part
to help the work along?
Or are you satisfied
to be the kind that just belongs?

Do you do your job well
and without a kick?
Or do you leave the work to just a few
and talk about the clique?

There's quite a program scheduled,
that I'm sure you've heard about.
And 'twill be appreciated, too,
if you will come help out.

Think this over, member
you know right from wrong.
Are you an active member,
or do you just belong?

A Wish for Leaders

I sincerely wish you will have the experience of thinking up a new idea, planning it, organizing it, and following it to completion and having it be magnificently successful. I also hope you'll go through the same process and have something bomb out.

I wish you could know how it feels "to run" with all your heart – and lose horribly.

I wish that you could achieve some great good for mankind, but have nobody know about it except you.

I wish you could find something so worthwhile that you deem it worthy of investing your life.

I hope you become frustrated and challenged enough to begin to push back the barriers of your own personal limitations.

I hope you make a stupid, unethical mistake and get caught red-handed and are big enough to say those magic words – I was wrong.

I hope you give so much of yourself that some days you wonder if it's worth it all.

I wish for you the worst kind of criticism for everything you do, because that makes you fight to achieve beyond what you normally would.

I wish for you the experience of leadership.

Affirmations

I am a miracle that can never be repeated.

I know who I am and where I am going.

I was created with a purpose and I am a valuable person.

I am full of energy.

I am responsible for my actions.

Love begins with me and I can give and receive love.

I believe in myself.

I am a strong and capable person.

I deserve the best life has to offer.

My self-discipline today will pay off tomorrow.

I will let go of the unwise choices of the past.

I am loving, kind, gentle and giving.

I was good today. I will be better tomorrow.

I have a sense of humor and can laugh at myself.

I am loved for who I am.

I am an open and caring person.

I am a positive person and surround myself with positive people.

I choose my attitude in every circumstance.

I am responsible for my feelings and actions.

I set the tone of a conversation with the tone of my voice.

I expect success.

I am no bigger than what it takes to upset me.

I accept people for who they are.

People need love the most when they are the most unlovable.

I am big enough to forgive anything.

Love is a decision and I have decided to love.

I see the best in people.

Every day in every way, I am getting better and better.

I have peace and love in my heart and it radiates from me.

Leadership

Is people,
the achievement
of goals,

Elections,
resources,
status,
and roles.

But more
than all others,
you'll have
to agree,

It's helping
and listening,
and calling us
WE.

Living and Giving

Whatever you give away today
or think or say or do
will multiply about tenfold
and then return to you.

It may not come immediately
nor from the obvious source,
but the LAW applies unfailingly
through some invisible force.

Whatever you feel about another,
be it love or hate or passion,
will surely bounce right back to you
in some clear or secret fashion.

If you speak about some person,
a word of praise or two,
soon tens of other people
will speak kind words of you.

Our thoughts are broadcasts of the soul,
not secrets of the brain.
Kind ones bring us happiness;
petty ones, untold pain?

Giving works as surely as
reflections in a mirror.
If hate you send, hate you'll get back . . .
But loving brings love nearer.

Remember as you start this day,
and duty crowds your mind,
that kindness comes so quickly back
to those who first are kind!

Let that thought and this one
direct you through each day . . .
the only things we ever keep
are the things we give away!

– Jerry Buchanan

Grades?

D   B   F   A+

    C-   D+   A-   B-

What the heck are all of these letters of the alphabet and symbols? Grades? No. These are letters of the alphabet randomly placed on this piece of paper. Some of the letters have plus or minus after them.

These aren't grades because no one has earned them.

You don't feel a sense of satisfaction for any work you've done by looking at the A-. You don't feel pride in this collection of letters and symbol.

Grades aren't just letters and symbols. Letters and symbols become grades when they are your personal return on the investment of your time and energy.

Grades aren't just what you see. Grades are what you EARN, and more important, what you FEEL.

Don't measure yourself by what you've accomplished, but by what you are capable of accomplishing with your ability.

> **"The greatest achievement of the human spirit is to live up to one's opportunities, and to make the most of one's resources."**
> **– Vauvenargues**

Leader Resolutions

No one will ever get out of this world alive.

RESOLVE therefore in the year to come to maintain a sense of values.

Take care of yourself. Good health is everyone's major source of wealth. Without it, happiness is almost impossible.

RESOLVE to be cheerful and helpful. People will repay you in kind. Avoid angry, abrasive persons. They are generally vengeful. Avoid zealots. They are generally humorless.

RESOLVE to listen more and talk less. No one ever learns anything by talking. Be chary of giving advice. Wise people don't need it, and fools won't heed it.

RESOLVE to be tender with the young, compassionate with the aged, sympathetic with the striving, and tolerant of the weak and the wrong.

Sometime in your life you will have been all of these. Do not equate money with success. There are many successful moneymakers who are miserable failures as human beings. What counts most about success is how one achieves it.

RESOLVE to love next year someone you didn't love this year. Love is the most enriching ingredient of life.

– Sir Walter Scott

Learners and Non-Learners

I don't divide the world into
        the weak and the strong,
Or the successes and failures,
        those that make it and those who don't.

I divide the world into
        the learners and the non-learners.
There are people who learn,
        who are open to what happens around them,
        who listen, who hear the lessons.

When they do something stupid,
        they don't do it again.
And when they do something that works a little bit,
        they do it even better and harder
        the next time.

The question to ask is not
        whether you are a success or a failure,
But whether you are a
        learner or non-learner.

— Benjamin Barber

Living Inside-Out

Living Inside-Out means not relying on praise and admiration from others to know you are doing what is right. It means being satisfied with your achievements from within.

Extreme materialism is a result of living the opposite way of life – living outside-in. People concerned with living outside-in believe they are less important than those around them. It's very important for these people to have the latest model of car, the trendiest clothes and expensive jewelry. Other people admire these material possessions. Materialistic people thrive on this recognition and admiration of their possessions. These people consider purchased items more important than what they have to offer as contributing human beings. Materialists magnify the purchasing or acquiring of possessions more than their own personal growth. Their approval comes from others.

When materialists are complimented, they usually elaborate on the comment. Rather than simply saying "thank you" and moving to more important conversation, they offer details about the item or how it was acquired. Compliments about possessions are successful parts of the materialists' days. Their attention is focused on the exterior world where each compliment is another form of acceptance by others.

Successful individuals living inside-out know they are valuable. Their passions and beliefs are not buried inside themselves. The negative labeling others often give is not a restricting factor for individuals living inside-out. They have listened to the disagreements and criticisms of others, but know these comments are responses to particular behaviors or situations, not to them.

Individuals living inside-out value themselves and others.

Like lobsters, which are vulnerable when they shed their protective shells, successful individuals are not afraid to be in potentially vulnerable situations. The risk of showing their inner self and not being accepted is considered small compared to the joy of sharing and growing with others. Successful individuals appreciate themselves and are not afraid of the acceptance of others.

Rather than being a leader, people living outside-in are followers. They do not recognize the priorities of what they want to accomplish. Instead, they are constantly watching everyone else and mocking the behavior of others. It is more important for them to be accepted. As a result, they imitate the behavior of others by following the latest trends and fads. These individuals have never found the secret of what makes them happy. Instead, they are always looking at outside forces to make them happy. They are searching outside themselves rather than looking within.

A famous philosopher said, *"The greatest challenge we have is that people do not know how to simply sit alone and be content anymore."* This statement reflects the challenges of materialists – people living outside-in.

It is not wrong or bad to possess material objects or want to enjoy modern conveniences. Only when the possessions become more important than ourselves should we be alarmed. Our contributions as helpful people to the betterment of ourselves and others are what matters. The number of items we own may be good for the jobs we help create and the convenience the goods provide. But above all other items in the world, people are the most important.

Consider...

What good is a beautiful, expensive gold necklace compared to sharing time with a lonely person?

Personal Challenges

A plane bound for Miami, Florida leaves Chicago, Illinois headed north. Headed north? How does the plane reach the southern state of Florida?

It may seem odd but planes often take-off in the opposite direction they are headed. The pilot simply readjusts the instruments to make the plane turn and travel south. Consider what is accomplished by these simple adjustments of the instruments in a big airplane. It is quite awesome.

There are many accounts of people whose lives seemed to be headed north when they wanted to head south. They were faced with enormous challenges and answered with awesome solutions. They accepted these circumstances as "challenges" to overcome rather than simply life's circumstances.

Consider these simple adjustments by ordinary people.

MELVILLE BISSEL of Grand Rapids, Michigan was a china dealer who suffered allergic headaches. The dusty packing straw used in the china trade aggravated his condition. To overcome this aggravation he invented and patented a carpet sweeper to scoop up the dust. His inventive contribution formed the Bissell Carpet Sweeper Company.

A print shop worker of Lowell, Massachusetts, HUMPHREY O'SULLIVAN, suffered from cramped and tired legs. He started using small rubber mats to ease the pain caused by standing on the hard concrete floors. O'Sullivan started nailing rubber patches on the bottom of his shoes after fellow workers walked off with the rubber mats. Once patented, the novel solution made O'Sullivan a very wealthy and comfortable man.

Rear Admiral GRACE MURRAY HOPPER was a pioneer in the computer industry. In fact, she was the third person to program the first computer which was 51 feet long, 8 feet high and 5 feet deep. Hopper became frustrated as more new software programs were written because each program included the same, repetitive machine instructions. To overcome this time-consuming process, she revolutionized computer software by inventing the first computer "compiler".

HENRY D. PERKY, lawyer and entrepreneur, was a victim of dyspepsia who wanted to develop a food that did not irritate his stomach. He began testing with wheat berry. The food grew in popularity and become a breakfast favorite. In 1930, the National Biscuit Company (Nabisco) bought the company which produced shredded wheat.

These people were faced with challenges. They made a difference for themselves and the world by positively meeting these personal challenges.

Your challenges may not be as dramatic, but they are important. Identify some part of your life that you want to improve and make it your personal challenge to make it better.

> **The reason a lot of people can't find opportunity is that it is often disguised as hard work.**

Thou Shalt Not Kill

We have human (and sometimes spiritual) laws that forbid us from killing others. These are easy laws to follow. Aren't they? You may say, Of course, I've never murdered another person. But what about…

- the enthusiasm of a committee member that vanished when the committee chair said his idea was bad?

- the smile of the sister that turned to a frown when her brother laughed at her new brightly colored dress?

- the wife's joy for a promotion that disappeared when her husband didn't congratulate him?

- the new member's timidness which increased when no one asked for his feedback?

- the man on the street who cheerfully said "hello" and was passed with no return acknowledgement?

- the young student who eagerly wanted to get involved but no one acknowledged his eagerness or abilities?

- the professor who was surprised when his "average" student received an A+ and suspiciously returned the student's test without a word of praise?

- the mother who told her son it was okay that he failed arithmetic because it had also been hard for her?

- the father who replied, "What a stupid question!" to his daughter.

- the man who hurriedly relayed a terrible rumor about a neighbor to everyone he met?

These situations occur every day. Unfortunately, all of us have harmed or killed someone's enthusiasm, attitude, reputation, expectations or joys. All of us are guilty. As a leader, your responsibility is to build others. Breathe life into others as an encourager and supporter.

Books that Build

This is a collection of wonderful messages I want to share with you. Some are very direct and others simply stories with magical words to ponder. Each book is fun-to-read and powerful in its own special way. Following each book is a brief explanation of the type of reading and focus. Those books with spiritual references have also been noted. Those marked by ** are highly recommended.

The quote *"Those who don't read are no better than those who can't,"* should be the theme for every breathing creature. We are what we think and what we think results from what we feed our minds.

Enjoy this smorgasbord of positive reading material as you pursue your personal leadership adventure!

The Alchemist – Paulo Coelho
(Best-selling story. Inspirational story of achieving our best.)

As A Man Thinketh – William James
(Classic Non-fiction. Self-esteem, goal setting & some spiritual references.)

Chicken Soup for the Soul – Jack Canfield & Mark Victor Hansen
(Best-selling collection of inspirational stories. Super resource for officers and some spiritual references.)

**CliftonStrengths for Students – Don Clifton with Gallup
(Non-fiction. Identifies your strengths and how to use them as you pursue your education.)

**Daring Greatly: How the Courage to be Vulnerable Transforms the Way We Live, Love, Parent and Lead – Brené Brown
(Best-selling Non-fiction. Self-esteem & authenticity)

**Drive – The Surprising Truth About What Motivates Us – Daniel Pink
(Best-selling Non-fiction. Wonderful collection of stories, research and ideas to use for personal and professional teams.)

**Fish: A Proven Way to Boost Morale and Improve Results – Stephen Lundin
(Best-selling Non-fiction. A parable that teaches engagement tools.)

Games Trainers Play Series – Newstrom & Scannell
(Group activities. Super resources for officers.)

The Giving Tree – Shel Silverstein
    (Children's story. Positive leadership message.)

**Habitudes Book #1: The Art of Self-Leadership [Values based] – Tim Elmore
    (Non-fiction. Leadership Principles shared with practical applications and
    beautiful pictures.)

Hope for the Flowers – Trina Paulus
    (Story. Positive messages. Appreciate your beauty & goal setting.)

**How Full is Your Bucket? – Tom Rath & Donald Clifton
    (Non-fiction. Includes a unique code to Clifton StrengthsFinder
    assessment.)

How Good Do We Have to Be? – Harold Kushner
    (Non-fiction. Self-esteem.)

**How to Win Friends and Influence People – Dale Carnegie
    (Non-fiction. Classic collection of success strategies & many quotes.)

**Leaders – Warren Bennis & Burt Nanus
    (Non-fiction. Leadership skills and some great quotes.)

**Leaders Eat Last: Why Some Teams Pull Together and Others Don't
    – Simon Sinek
    (Non-fiction. Leadership Skills & Team Building)

**Let Your Life Speak – Parker Palmer
    (Non-fiction. Discovering your purpose.)

Made to Stick – Chip and Dan Heath
    (Non-fiction. Developing quality ideas that connect.)

Mastery – George Leonard
    (Non-fiction. Positive attitude & goal setting.)

On Becoming a Leader – Warren Bennis
    (Non-fiction. Leadership skills & some great quotes.)

**The Precious Present – Spencer Johnson
    (Story. Positive message & value for the present.)

Principled Centered Leadership – Stephen Covey
    (Non-fiction. Goal-setting, leadership skills, some great quotes & some
    spiritual references.)

<u>Psychology of Winning</u> – Denis Waitley
>(Non-fiction. Self-esteem, great quotes/stories & some spiritual references.)

<u>See You At The Top</u> – Zig Ziglar
>(Non-fiction. Goal setting & some spiritual references.)

**<u>The Servant. A Simple Story About Leadership</u> – James Hunter
>(Non-fiction. Wonderful story about servant leadership.)

**<u>Seven Habits of Highly Effective People</u> – Stephen Covey
>(Non-fiction. Goal setting, self-esteem, time management, some spiritual references and tremendous stories.)

**<u>Strengths Based Leadership: Great Leaders, Teams & Why People Follow</u>
>- Tom Rath (Non-fiction. Leadership, Motivation & Strengths)

<u>True Success</u> – Tom Morris, Ph.D.
>(Non-fiction. Goal setting, motivation & self-esteem.)

<u>What to Say When You Talk to Yourself</u> – Shad Helmstetter
>(Non-fiction. Self-esteem & some spiritual references.)

**<u>Who I Am Depends on Me!</u> – Patty Hendrickson
>(Non-fiction. Self-esteem, leadership skills & some great quotes.)

<u>"Yes" or "No"</u> – Spencer Johnson
>(Story. Decision-making.)

<u>You Can If You Think You Can</u> – Norman Vincent Peale
>(Non-fiction. Classic book. Positive attitude, self-esteem, goal setting, great quotes/stories & some spiritual references.)

Hope you find these wonderful messages inspirational as you begin exploring yourself and discovering your tremendous potential. My search for new, exciting resources is continuous. If you have read something wonderful, please share it with me at Patty@pattyhendrickson.com.

> **"Your mind stretched to a new idea,
> Never goes back to its original dimension."
> – Oliver Wendell Holmes**

Points to Ponder
Stuff I Know To Be True

When you are feeling very stressed and want to release an emotion or get angry. Stop. Breathe. The few moments you wait could save you both embarrassment and possibly damaged relationships.

Use the "Grandma Test" when you post anything online. The Grandma Test is simply, "Would you be proud to have your grandma see what you posted?" If not, it is not appropriate.

Remember, once you post something online it is there FOREVER – that's a long time.

The greatest thing you can do in any presentation is thoroughly prepare.

Always choose to dress a bit dressier when you aren't certain what to wear. You don't have the opportunity to re-make your first impression.

Nearly every item of clothing looks better without wrinkles. Learn how to use an iron or steamer and use it often!

Use the plastic dry cleaning bags around your clothes in your suitcase when traveling. It prevents the clothes from wrinkling.

When someone says they are going to "Wing it" what they are really saying is "I'm not going to invest the time to make this as good as it could be." Ultimately, they are cheating themselves out of developing their skills as much as they could. They are also cheating the recipients of the presentation because they aren't doing their best.

Respect the personal challenges of others and be appreciative of all they are able to contribute to the team.

Whoever is comfortable with the silence in most negotiations has the real power. Don't feel the need to fill silence.

You are the best officer the day you give up your office.

Try not to say "You don't have the time." If you invest just 20-minutes every day doing something you enjoy, in one year you've invested 7,300 minutes in this activity. That equals more than 121 hours or more than five days of time you invest in this activity. Small bits of time add up. Use yours wisely.

Don't complain about your job. You are paid for your efforts. If you don't like it, find another one.

A smile on your face literally gives you energy. Resist the urge to frown or scowl. Instead, smile!

If you're at a meal function and feeling a bit uncomfortable or uneasy, turn the focus away from your nervousness. Instead, make it your mission to make everyone at the table comfortable. Make certain you ask every person a question to include them in conversation. Your graciousness will be noticed and appreciated.

Always remember your "PLEASE" and ""THANK YOU's". You stand out when you regularly use your good manners.

Before judging someone or something, first consider where that person or circumstance comes from. When we first look to understand someone else's history we open our eyes to the bigger world and possibilities.

When someone invites you to make a presentation and gives you a time frame. Always stay within the time frame. In fact, make notations on your notes for parts of the presentation you could eliminate if you needed to shorten the presentation.

Those individuals who make fun of someone's accent should stop and consider the situation. The person with the accent probably knows at least two languages. How many languages do you speak?

Try to carry items in your left hand. You never know when you will meet someone. It's nice to easily have your right hand available to shake hands with the other person without jostling things from one arm or hand to the other.

When you are invited to speak always ask who is speaking before and after you and how the transitions will be handled.

One of the greatest gifts you can give your organization is to seek out those individuals to replace you in the future. It is sometimes called succession planning. Ultimately it builds the leadership of your organization and makes people feel empowered when you recognize and encourage them as potential future elected leaders. Plant the seeds of encouragement for those who could run for office.

Texting when you are talking with someone else is often considered downright rude.

Be on time!

Celebrate the success of others. Make a point to often send congratulation notes, texts and e-mails to others.

Other people want to know that their opinion matters. Make eye contact with as many people as possible to build an inclusive atmosphere.

If you forget someone's name, don't be embarrassed. Simply say something polite like, "I remember smiling at you (or shaking hands with you) (or something else about your previous encounter), I'm (share your name)." The other person will usually shake hands and share their name with you. It's a pleasant way to reconnect.

Get the business cards of others when you have a situation that you want to learn more about. If you have the other person's card and your interest is high, you know you will make the contact. Giving someone else your card and asking them to follow-up with you doesn't guarantee they will.

Brush your teeth and comb, brush, fluff, or pick your hair.

Have at least two favorite quotes handy to use. You never know when you'll be asked to speak or write a short article on the spot.

It's always better to under-promise and over-deliver, rather than over-promise and under-deliver.

We are all at different levels of readiness.

When you are asked to make decisions on behalf of your membership, remember the wide variety of your membership – ages, tenure, geography, socio-economic status, involvement – before you cast your vote. You are a representative acting on behalf of many others. What a privilege!

It's important to recognize the support of others.

Don't complain about your officer or leadership duties. Remember that you were probably elected and someone else didn't receive enough votes. You wanted that job and you said you would do a good job. Those other officer candidates would be happy and proud to fulfill those duties that you are complaining about.

Try to arrive at events well-rested. You'll do a better job and appreciate the experience much more.

Check your facts.

Commit to being a good listener as often as possible. Really listen to the voice, the face, the body, the tone and the energy. People will feel your attentiveness.

Be nice. The world needs more kind people. Be the example.

This is a good start. You will continue to have "aha" moments throughout your leadership experience. I hope you take time to reflect, particularly after a challenging situation. Actively look for the learning point. What have you gleaned from the experience? Write it down as part of this section. Let it be your Points to Ponder or This Stuff I Know To Be True. Good Luck!!

_____

_____

_____

_____

_____

_____

_____

_____

_____

_____

_____

_____

_____

Keepers

This leadership guide was written with the hope that you would feel empowered to explore your gifts and enthusiastically embark on your leadership journey. This collection of ideas is only the start. I hope you circle, highlight, underline or draw stars around the content that really resonates with you. I hope you use this guide as a stepping stone to even more discoveries and experiences.

We've included several Keeper Pages. This is where you write down great quotes your hear; books people recommend; videos you want to watch; outstanding podcasts and so much more. This guide works when you work with it.

Best wishes as you unpack, explore and grow the magic that is you!!

Keepers

Keepers

Keepers

Made in the USA
Monee, IL
13 July 2021